Published by Philoptima, llc.

Copyright © by Byron Harrell

All rights reserved.

Published in the United States and Canada by Philoptima, llc.
New Orleans, Louisiana

www.philoptima.org

Philoptima is a registered trademark.

Library of Congress
Harrell, Byron, 2009
LCCN: 2009901678

Supercharged Giving:
The Professional's Guide to Strategic Philanthropy / Byron Harrell

ISBN 978-0-9821077-8-2

1.   Philanthropy-Strategic Targeting- Planning-New Orleans-
Examples.   2. Professional Guide-Strategic Giving. 3. Con-
cept Mapping-Graphic Language Terminology. 4. Donations-
Impact-National-Examples. 5. Philoptima-Supercharged Giving.
SAN: 857-2836

Dust Jacket Design: Pieter Tandjung

Manufactured in the United States of America

First Edition
2009

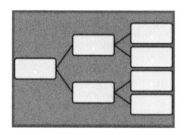

PRAISE FOR
Dr. Byron Harrell
and
Supercharged Giving

The Professional's Guide To Strategic Philanthropy

"*Supercharged Giving* should be required reading for every person entering the foundation world - and a handy refresher for the veterans. Concept Mapping deserves a "good housekeeping seal of approval!" The "*Key Points to Remember*" are solid reference points and formatted in a way that makes future scanning easy.

Debra Jacobs, President

The Patterson Foundation, Sarasota

"Coming from an experienced foundation executive, Dr. Harrell's message to donors is an urgent call for strategic focus and clarity in grantmaking which should be high on our list if we are to stay relevant in our communities for the long haul. "

Ford Weber, Executive Director

Virginia LISC, Richmond

"Dr. Harrell, your work is not only thoughtful, but clearly on point for those grantmakers who are well meaning yet not clear on how to optimize their good heart and generosity. And it is a great refinement tool even for those philanthropists who have been around for generations."

Donald Smithburg, Principal

Health Management Associates, Chicago

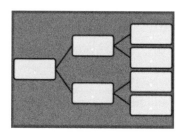

Dedicated to those who give
of themselves and their treasure
for the benefit of others,
asking nothing in return.

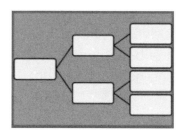

Supercharged Giving:
The Professional's Guide to Strategic Philanthropy

Preface

Amidst an economic melt-down of epic proportions, philanthropists are dialing down their giving and looking for more value and impact from their grantmaking. With deeply reduced endowments, they can no longer afford a scattergun approach to their donations. Now, more than ever, donors are designing thoughtful strategic approaches to their work that achieve more impact for each grant dollar. For grantmakers looking for the path to a more strategic, cost-effective style of philanthropy *Supercharged Giving* offers a balanced approach between art and science. It also proposes a new way to link each grant to the reasoning and logic of the funder known as "Concept Mapping".

This is a practical "how to" book from an experienced philanthropist. It is designed to give funders a way to balance their analytical tendencies with their heart-felt passion to help others. Some believe that philanthropy is in danger of losing respect for simple acts of charity in favor of complex theories of change and grantmaking logic models. Others believe that philanthropy is peppered with dilatants that are inattentive to measurable outcomes. *Supercharged Giving* proposes a novel way to think about philanthropy strategically without letting the passionate overwhelm the analytical; the heart overwhelm the mind.

The analytical "mind" side of philanthropy is being shaped by leading strategists such as Michael Porter, Phil Buchanan, Joel Fleishman, Mark Kramer, Peter Frumkin, Paul Brest, and Hal Harvey. They have each written powerfully about the frequently observed failure of philanthropy to achieve durable, lasting results. Theirs is a well developed body of knowledge offering different but equally intriguing approaches to the challenges of effectively using private wealth for the public good.

The passionate "heart" side of philanthropy is promoted by other leaders such as Pablo Eisenberg, Martin Lehfeldt, and William Schambra who suggest that philanthropists hang onto the beliefs that motivate them and keep things simple and focused. They note that philanthropy is littered with fads and flashy trends that all too frequently have not improved grantmaking outcomes.

Supercharged Giving blends these two approaches to grantmaking. Using a powerful new tool known as "Concept Mapping" philanthropists are able to clearly document their grantmaking rationale and their impact can be kicked up a notch without smothering their underlying motivations. Concept Mapping is a very robust tool that helps grantmakers make sense of why they give and the result they want. It also graphically demonstrates their reasoning and provides a great communication tool that helps them stay the course when working with grantees, partners, the public and regulators. Creating a Concept Map forces philanthropists to prioritize their limited resources, establish a working knowledge in their targeted field, and craft a game plan to guide their work. A Concept Map helps remind funders and grantees alike why they support a given intervention and how success will be measured across time. Finally, Concept Mapping captures, in a single graphic, a whole portfolio of diverse projects that might otherwise appear disconnected, but which make sense viewed collectively as a single theory of change.

To the extent that business-like strategies and Concept Mapping contribute to more understandable and effective grantmaking, this author will be gratified. My hope is that "mapping" will encourage donors to be more precise about why they are making grants, what they expect to accomplish, and more understandable to their grantees and communities.

With diligence, donors can find the perfect balance between their minds and their hearts; the analytical and the charitable. *Supercharged Giving* presents a wide range of grantmaking styles and approaches, at least a few of which should work for you and your organization. Achieving a bigger, lasting impact is all about connecting the ideas...and the boxes.

TABLE OF CONTENTS

	Page
Introduction	1
PART ONE	5
Chapter One Strategic Imperative	6
Chapter Two Deciding "What" To Do	15
Chapter Three Deciding "Why" To Do It	29
Chapter Four Deciding "How" To Do It	37
PART TWO	45
Chapter Five Strategic Cycle: Analysis & Input	47
Chapter Six Strategic Design	55
Chapter Seven Implementation	61
Chapter Eight Monitor Programs & Results	69
Chapter Nine Evaluate & Adjust	75
PART THREE	89
Chapter Ten Grantmaking Processes, Products & Styles	91
Chapter Eleven Concept Mapping© for Grantmakers	105
Chapter Twelve Other Uses of Concept Mapping©	137
Chapter Thirteen Conclusion	149
Appendix Nominal Group Technique	153
END NOTES	161
SPECIAL BONUS REPORT: **Why Big Foundations Perform Poorly**	177

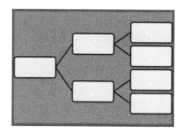

Introduction

Most Americans are "philanthropists" to one degree or another. They drop a coin in the kettle during the holidays, they give time to help clear an elderly neighbor's driveway, or they give thousands or even millions to nonprofits to help the less fortunate. Their collective charitable impulse has amazed observers from the earliest years of the nation and they continue to share their wealth and energies today.

Although they may not always think of themselves as philanthropists, they possess the three essential elements of philanthropy including (1) time, energy, or wealth to share with others, (2) motivation to give, and (3) belief that their gifts will have an impact.

Supercharged Giving is devoted to maximizing the third element: "impact". Donors must believe that their gifts will have an impact or they wouldn't make them. In Part One of *Supercharged Giving*, donors are guided to answer three questions that are fundamentally important to high-impact philanthropy.

(1) "<u>What</u> do you want to accomplish with your gift(s)?",

(2) "<u>Why</u> do you want to achieve a particular result?", and

(3) "<u>How</u> will you achieve the result you seek?".

Because the answers to these three questions are essential to the creation of a meaningful concept map, *Supercharged Giving* devotes a separate chapter to each question and each chapter includes a "family" of related decisions that collectively guide the donor's strategies.

In Part Two, *Supercharged Giving* proposes that funders adopt a strategic planning cycle that requires them to revisit these three questions as part of their annual business process.

In Part Three, funders are introduced to a range of grant products and grantmaking styles and an important new communication tool known as "Concept Mapping". "Mapping" helps them keep their day-to-day decisions consistent with their long range goals and helps them avoid "mission drift" which is a common philanthropic malady. The ability to plan for the long haul while maximizing impact in the short term is critically important to funders with scarce resources. *Supercharged Giving* is an invaluable reference to keep funders on course throughout the year and each time a funder wants to tackle a new community challenge. A business plan built on the principals enumerated in this book will help ensure that day-to-day decisions are tightly integrated into the big picture and it will help avoid retracing wasteful, nonproductive work.

Concept Mapping is useful to donors with large or small endowments. It can be applied to simple projects or to complex, multi-year initiatives. Concept Mapping documents what, why, and how a particular grant (or portfolio of several grants) has been implemented from among several differing alternatives. As a communication tool, it provides a pictorial mechanism for readers to quickly grasp the theoretical connections between the mission of the foundation or the intent of the donor and a specific gift or grant.

From the completely opposite viewpoint of nonprofit organizations which receive gifts, Concept Mapping can be helpful in designing programs and interventions that are attractive to donors. In such a "reverse engineering" approach, nonprofits can start with the outcomes and impacts of their programs and map backwards to demonstrate the linkages between their work and the goals of funders. Thus, by using Concept Mapping, nonprofits can approximate the reasoning of funders.

For consultants, planners, experts, and advisors to foundations, *Supercharged Giving* is a valuable guide to help their clients answer the "what", "why", and "how" questions of strategic philanthropy. Professionals using annual strategic planning cycles and Concept Mapping will find these to be useful tools to assist their foundation clients adopt more sophisticated, effective grant making approaches.

Supercharged Giving describes several different grantmaking styles and different types of grants that can be matched to donors to enhance their impact. Most grantmakers use just one style of giving even if they offer several different types of grants (i.e. core-support grants or capital grants). However, a foundation can intentionally use a different grant-making style for each type of grant they issue.

By adopting different styles, grantmakers can vary their reasoning, measurement, and evaluation approaches to a grant. As an example, "discretionary donations" (small charitable grants with very simple application forms and few or no reports required from the recipient) can be issued to grantees under a "venturist" style and should be measured very differently than the same type of grant delivered under an "altruist" style. The expectations are different for each style.

Supercharged Giving contains practical techniques to assess the environment, establish goals, strategies, objectives, adopt grant products and styles, and build clear, flexible grantmaking approaches. It includes clear explanations and illustrations covering aspects of defining, developing, and implementing a strategic philanthropic business plan. It even explores different grant implementation options and includes two different examples that apply the concepts presented in this book.

Supercharged Giving is the professional's essential guide to strategic philanthropy and Concept Mapping.

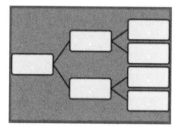

PART ONE

1. Strategic Imperative

2. "What" To Do

3. "Why" Do It

4. "How" To Do It

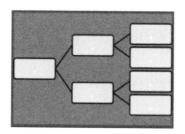

CHAPTER ONE

Strategic Imperative

Faust made a pact with the devil and was granted energy, life, knowledge, and youth to his utmost happiness. In exchange, all Faust was required to do was avoid wishing that things would never change. After he unwittingly tripped over this simple prohibition, his world and his life were thrown to the devil (Mephistopheles) whereupon he ruined the lives of those whom he loved. His life ended in shame. Faust constantly sought perfection but never found it (1). Similarly, philanthropists seek but never find perfection having made two Faustian bargains of their own (2).

In the first "bargain", philanthropists receive tax deductions in exchange for committing their private wealth to the service of the public good. The donor also retained control over how the donated assets were used (often across multiple generations). Measured in purely financial terms, the first "bargain" has been a wildly successful public policy. It has produced an ocean of tax-free assets approaching $600 billion held in more than 70,000 private foundations. However, the first "bargain" has not been without a few trade-offs for society such as reduced government income and deferred impact. In addition, the public has little influence over the investment, spending, or grantmaking choices of foundations because their endowments remain privately owned but publicly dedicated.

In the second "bargain" foundations received freedom from almost any oversight. In return for their tax-deductible gifts, donors were permitted to direct grants to almost any nonprofit cause with a prohibition against lobbying and another against self-dealing. With so few external controls, foundation grant making can often appear messy and idiosyncratic. As a consequence, vast sums have been spent to improve society with seemingly very little effort to plan for, strategize over, or evaluate results (3). Thus, foundation spending can run the gamut from the arts to zoology and everything in between without any evidence required of social impact, good, bad, or otherwise.

Even with so much at risk, Faust tragically slipped into the grasp of the devil. So go foundations that fail to pay their excise taxes or that trip over lobbying or self-dealing restrictions. But bureaucratic death sentences have been rare. Unlike Faust, private foundations can still get away with wishing that things would never change and some things don't as evidenced by their spending, which can remain stuck in outmoded and overly simplistic practices (4).

Donors have also become accustomed to working without any accepted yardstick to measure how or even if they are succeeding. Without this feedback system, foundation spending can be stuck in patterns that worked in the 1950's but are ineffective in tackling today's problems. Many foundations have been forced to improvise and to develop their own home-grown evaluation techniques and tools to measure their performance. But, the use of sophisticated tools has been limited, and, to date, there have been few mechanisms through which to share grant making results.

No other large-scale corporate activity in the United States functions with as little regulatory oversight, as few indicators of success, and as much insulation from criticism as philanthropy (5). Indeed, philanthropists have created some of the best and worst institutions in American society (6). To their credit, philanthropists have shown bursts of ingenuity and responsiveness accompanied by lasting and positive impact on society (4; 8).

Two modern examples among many are the scholars program for authoritative field research supported by the Russell Sage Foundation and the VERA Institute's program targeting the criminal justice system supported by the Ford Foundation (9; 10). Others include the national youth anti-smoking campaign funded by the Robert Wood Johnson Foundation or the Sustainable Environment Program funded by the

Pew Charitable Trusts both of which have been credited with changing public attitudes toward recognition of large-scale hazards (8).

While grant effectiveness has largely been viewed through the eye of the beholder, from an outsider's perspective, there are also ample examples that donors don't always make "good" grants and waste vast sums of money with little or no effect (7). As examples of dubious funding, Wooster points to the support by the Ford and Carnegie Foundations for public television and to the "war on cancer" funded by the Albert and Mary Lasker Foundation which greatly expanded federal pending (7). A more modern example could be the uninspiring results noted by Fleishman of the *Living Cities* (formerly NCDI) housing program funded by an unprecedented collaboration of private and governmental entities but whose shifting approaches, unclear results, and vague theories over time serve as reminders of the importance of consistent strategic focus (8).

Unfortunately, undisciplined spending has been easily justified in an equally undisciplined field. As a result, many observers of philanthropy have come to believe that foundation spending produces fewer lasting positive effects than should be expected (3). On one hand, some suggest that the whole concept of strategic philanthropy or even of professionalism in the field is without merit (11); while, on the other hand, some suggest that the root of philanthropic ineffectiveness may rest in the failure of the field to adopt more structured and systematic approaches (8; 12).

As an example, of the thirteen most common reasons for foundation failure noted by Dr. Joel Fleishman in his book "The Foundation", half are rooted in weak systems (2007). Specifically, he notes that failure rests in (1) a lack of a guiding strategy, (2) a mismatch between the problem and the strategy, (3) a lack of a credible logic model, (4) a failure to specify precise desired outcomes, (5) inadequate market research, and (6) a lack of appreciation for unanticipated consequences (8). In response, donors have turned to strategic philanthropy to boost their effectiveness.

While there is little doubt that charitable acts in general are good for both the donor and society, a widely held viewpoint has evolved in the field that "charity" is a lesser form of a more sophisticated philanthropy (13). Strategic philanthropy is the term often used to describe a business-like model of giving that is part venture capitalist and part demanding investor that aligns the goals and objectives of the donor with the activities of the grantee (14).

Yet, it can also be argued that a purely business-like approach to giving can leave the donor and the grantee financially or spiritually impoverished (13). Another debate rages between others who believe that the passion of the donor is at the heart of great philanthropy and those who believe that those same passions are too narrow and unsupported, to make lasting and important differences to society (8; 13; 15). *Supercharged Giving* proposes a middle ground between "red hot" passion and "ice cold" strategy. By using a traditional business model for strategic planning that is wedded to a simple graphic language called "concept mapping", it is possible to achieve more effective results without losing sight of the original impulse of the donor or the needs of the targeted community.

Philanthropy will undoubtedly remain a field dominated by these two camps--those who believe in a structured process and those who believe in the individualistic passions of giving. Both viewpoints have a legitimate place in philanthropy. *Supercharged Giving* proposes that these two viewpoints are different but operate on the same linear scale of grant making styles of giving, from more sophisticated to less sophisticated. The practitioners of either viewpoint will discover that a systematic measurable approach will not necessarily extinguish important passions. Instead, grantmakers of all stripes are likely to find that they can purchase greater impact for the same or fewer dollars by applying a strategic approach to grantmaking and they can still maintain balance between passion and analysis.

Getting Things Done vs. Doing The Right Thing

Because foundations enjoy unfettered freedom to act and very little external accountability, it can be difficult for them to identify the work that is most important, and, it is even more difficult for them to stay focused on their goals over time. In order to cope with this issue, they often develop complex systems and procedures that belie the fact that they may be guilty of wandering, whimsical decision-making.

Rather than wrestle with the "mission-drift" dilemma, some philanthropists begin to place an inordinate emphasis on the processes they employ; they fail to understand that the choice of a specific gift shouldn't be merely a mechanical by-product of the process (16). They have created intricately detailed applications and guidelines, procedures to rank the relative worth of proposals, and tightly written performance contracts. These procedures can be multi-layered involving staff, consultants, committee members, the board of directors and even non-voting advisory members of the public. Completing all of the procedures becomes the mission, rather than the procedures serving as merely a useful technique to achieve the real mission.

The larger the foundation, the more internal structures and processes seem to take control and dominate foundation operations. The diminished focus on important outcomes has caused many large foundations to become low-performing organizations (18). The simple proposition that grant spending should have a logically anticipated outcome established by the founder or board somehow gets lost in the process (4).

Bureaucracy being what it is, over time the emphasis has subtly shifted from the process driving the grantmaking decision to the process itself becoming paramount. Rather than the foundation using the process to find the right answer for the community, it simply finds an answer that has all of the boxes checked and the forms completed (17). The "proceduralists" have built increasingly complex systems to prove their added value, but which act as ramparts that have the unintended consequence of keeping small or unsophisticated applicants from seeking funding. The mechanics of processing applications, filing reports, sending checks, conducting site visits, and pouring over audits and evaluation data supports a feeling of "getting things done" rather than "doing the right things".

Strategic Philanthropy Defined

In business, a strategy maps out the organization's future, setting out which products and services a company will take to market (19). A similar strategy for grantmaking foundations has been described as the reasoning behind how a particular goal should be achieved and is often used interchangeably with the term "theory of change" (20; 21). Philanthropists who set out clear goals and objectives are relatively rare and even fewer are those who attempt to explain why they believe that a particular activity will produce a particular result (22; 23). Foundations that develop a theory of change to undergird their grantmaking approach do not simply hand out money. Rather, they attach their own set of assumptions and expected outcomes to their grants (24).

Image 1: Some Foundations Are Simply Lost

Why Can't We Just Google It?

Among foundations that use a strategic approach to produce social improvement, strategies are most often based on a combination of objective evidence drawn from the literature and subjective assumptions of causality (23). Some argue that a strategic approach to grantmaking offers little improvement over an expressed ideology because there is a lack of empirical evidence of causal relationships. While causality is often unproven, strategic philanthropy makes a meaningful attempt to understand how and why change occurs. Foundations that adopt a strategic approach are likely to improve the effectiveness of their grantmaking (8). For purposes of *Supercharged Giving*, strategic philanthropy has been defined as follows (25; 26).

Definition 1: Strategic Philanthropy

> **Strategic philanthropy** is a dynamic process which blends the art and science of grantmaking to produce a written plan that governs how the foundation uses its monetary and human capital to achieve its mission.

In the next three chapters, *Supercharged Giving* answers the timeless grantmaking questions of "what", "why" and "how" followed by chapters covering the description of a strategic planning cycle and Concept Mapping.

Key Points To Remember:

• Private foundations enjoy no inherent right to exist. They are creatures of the tax code and as such operate at the mercy of the Congress and the IRS.

• There are more than 70,000 private foundations today and the assets of private foundations total nearly $600 billion.

• As a group, foundations operate without any accepted standards of performance and thus have a difficult time gauging success.

• Many grantmakers have turned to increasingly complex bureaucratic processes in lieu of measuring their impact.

• The passion of the founder or the board for a particular subject is often not enough to produce meaningful results. There is an appropriate balance between passion and bureaucracy.

• Large foundations are more likely to be ineffective.

• Strategic philanthropy is a dynamic process which blends the art and science of grantmaking to produce a written plan that governs how the foundation uses its monetary and human capital to achieve its mission.

CHAPTER TWO

Deciding "What" To Do

Most foundations have a mission that describes what they do. Settling on "What" to do is the result of a series of conclusions known in *Supercharged Giving* as the "What To Do" family of decisions. The mission of the foundation, its goals, and its objectives are all in the "What" family. Funders also work through two other series of conclusions known as the "Why Do It" and the "How To Do It" families.

The "Why" family defines success for the organization and becomes the basis of its vision. The "How" family includes strategies, theories of change, tactics, logic models, action steps, and budgets. Together, answers to these three questions, "What", "Why", and "How", form the strategic plan for the organization. Of the three questions, "What To Do" is the most important. The board of directors is essential to finding the answer to this critically important question.

Do not rush through this chapter just because you already have a mission! The single most important step in strategic philanthropy, and the one with the greatest long-term effect, is the decision of "What To Do". The answer to the "What" question is the mission.

Graphic 1: A Question Of Leadership

The Board or Founder
Leads the Way

What To Do:

Mission, Goals &   **Desired**
Objectives   **Outcome**

Why Do It

How To Do It:

Strategies (Theories of Change)

Tactics   (Logic Models)

Getting It Done:

Measuring, Monitoring, Evaluation

Definition 2: What Is A Mission Statement?

> **The mission** of a foundation is a broad description of its reason for existence with sufficiently measurable terms or sub-sets (goals) that the long term success of the organization can be assessed.

Few established foundations ever re-examine their overarching purpose. After all, the answer to the "what" question was laid out by the founder. Newly formed foundations pay a little more attention to the "what to do" question but with the passage of time they also rarely question the appropriateness of their first answer.

There are three steps to developing a good philanthropic mission.

1. Identifying the problem to be confronted,

2. Fitting the mission to the organization, and,

3. Writing the mission statement.

Graphic 2: The Most Important Questions In Philanthropy

What To Do & Why ?

<u>MISSION</u>   **Desired Outcome**

Everything else is about
How to do it ?

Before taking the first step to develop a philanthropic mission, there are a few broad issues to consider. In spite of its importance, the mission is often written in vague, poetic, sweeping language because generations of executives have been *wrongly* taught by business schools that the mission of an organization is a quasi-permanent, essentially immutable declaration of purpose. As a result, this vital guiding statement is given scant attention during the strategic planning process in most established organizations in favor of jumping straight into the details.

It is true that the mission changes less frequently than very detailed quarterly action steps. However, it is untrue that it should be static and it is unwise in a dynamic environment to think that it should be. Consequently, many grants issued by foundations are less effective than they could be because of this unwarranted inflexibility combined with vague, beguiling terms.

Sometimes called "donor intent", the mission of a private foundation should not be fixed in perpetuity simply because the organization itself is perpetual or because of a long-departed donor. It seems obvious that the problems being confronted by a perpetual organization should not be confined to outdated assumptions from its distant past. Founders may operate with a superficial understanding of the issues that influence the problem they have chosen to solve or how to measure its causes, scope, and complexity. This is where founders get derailed and many of them never regain their forward momentum. Consequently, even after years of grantmaking, many funders are unable to determine if they have made any lasting progress.

Supercharged Giving suggests that this aversion to amending the mission or re-defining donor intent is harmful to foundations and the communities they serve. Problems do not stand still over time and neither should solutions! Instead, this book proposes a structured re-examination of each level of the "What To Do" family of decisions. The following terms are discussed in detail in later chapters, but for now, imagine that every level of "What" decision-making is strictly confined. *By definition*, once all action plans are achieved, the objective associated with those action plans is also finished. *By definition*, once all objectives are achieved, the goal associated with those objectives is also completed. *By definition,* once all goals are completed, the mission is accomplished. As a result, every level of decision-making in the "What" family is systematically subjected to re-examination, including the mission. Action plans may be revised quarterly, objectives may be revised annually, goals may be revised every few years, and the mission may be fundamentally revisited every 5-8 years. Ultimately, this approach helps the funder to remain relevant in changing times.

Most private foundations, unlike their founders, will be around forever. What happens to the foundation if it achieves all of the goals established by its founder? Founders rarely thought about the role of the foundation once it achieved the purpose for which it was created. Thus, they often chose impossible-to-measure, overly broad missions. *Supercharged Giving* proposes that a more appropriate mission designed for a perpetual-life organization favors the adoption of a mission that is relatively "temporary" and more responsive to external conditions.

Start At The Beginning

Foundations should take the time and make the effort to carefully define their mission in measureable, clear terms. Armed with a precise mission or statement of purpose, grantmakers can focus their efforts. A clear mission also provides a defensive barrier to protect against "mission drift". Alfred P. Sloan (science & technology) and Robert Wood Johnson (health) serve as striking examples of donors who forcefully imbedded a clear focus in their missions and thus prevented future generations of leaders from watering down their work and from a lack of accountability for results (8; 13). Tom Peters called this clarity of purpose "sticking to their knitting" in his famously successful business tome "In Search of Excellence" (27). He noted that few, if any, of the best companies in the world deliver consistently good products or services under vague or inconsistent goals. The same principle holds true for foundations and other donors.

Although there are striking differences between business enterprises and nonprofit organizations, they must both add value for their constituents (28). Thus, creating a strong, clear mission builds a walled fortress for the organization that accomplishes at least two very important purposes: (1) it helps applicants, grantees, and communities understand the focal point of the foundation, and, (2) it protects the foundation from itself by confining it inside the mission walls to remain attentive to a few important activities until something is accomplished.

Step One: Identifying The Problem

Brest and Harvey propose three interacting scales to guide the selection of a philanthropic mission (29). They suggest a three-dimensional balancing act that considers (1) the scale or the size of the problem that the funder is attempting to solve, (2) the degree of permanence of the harm caused by the problem, and (3) the impact of the problem on the quality of life.

This approach is constructive in that it produces information about the scope of effort that may be required by a philanthropist to attack a particular problem. With some modification to fit philanthropy as envisioned in *Supercharged Giving*, the following three scales may be a useful way to explore the "What To Do" question.

1. What Is The Scale of The Issue?

The following scale helps frame the size or breadth of the problem that the funder wants to solve. It ranges from a small-impact problem to a large-impact problem (Brest uses the term "vast").Other units of measure in this scale are possible such as money, acres of land, people, or even ratios such as income per capita but the central idea is to understand the magnitude.

Graphic 3: Problem Identification Model

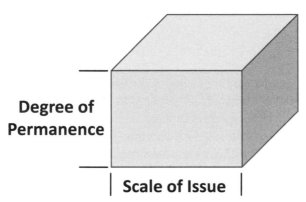

Systemic Mission Balancing

Degree of Permanence

| Scale of Issue |

Graphic 4: How Big Is The Problem Being Confronted?

Small   Medium   Large

The scale of the issue helps bring a touch of reality to the expansiveness of the philanthropist's choice of mission and to the descriptive language that will be used to describe the challenge.

2. What Is The Degree Of Permanent Harm?

This scale measures the temporary or permanent nature of the harm being created by the issue under consideration by the grantmaker. When dealing with the consequences of postponing action, grantmakers can consider just how reversible are the consequences produced by the issue of interest, some of which can last years or even decades. Some problems left unresolved can produce irreversible harm. Thus, a scale of "degree of permanence" runs from short-term to long-term; reversible to irreversible.

Graphic 5: How Reversible Are The Affects Of The Problem?

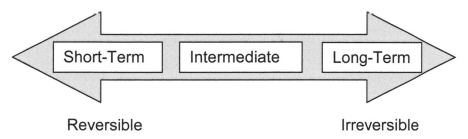

If the consequence of postponing action is negligible, the short-term (reversible) side of the scale is applicable. If the problem is left unattended and the consequences are irreversible such as cutting down the last stand of centuries-old red wood trees, the long-term or irreversible measure on the right side of the scale is more appropriate.

3. What Is The Level Of Threat From The Problem?

If the problem being considered as one basis for the mission reduces the quality of life, this third scale captures the effect. In the middle of the scale, the problem negatively affects the necessities of life and on the far right end of the scale are those problems that threaten life itself.

Graphic 6: Impact On Quality Of Life

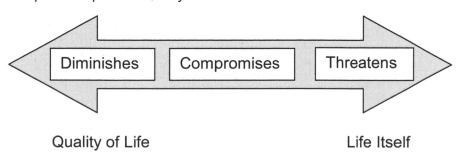

These three scales describe a framework for the consideration of large-scale issues that a philanthropist considers when establishing or when re-appraising the mission of the foundation. The larger the problem being addressed, the more the mission should be written in global terms to describe very large-scale challenges that may last for several generations. A good example of a super-sized mission is "the elimination of HIV" or of "poverty". A precautionary note, working at the outer ends of these three scales generally requires more money and a great deal of patience and persistence. This "big-box" work can also be difficult to measure and a myriad of complex issues can be expected to interrupt progress. Additionally, success is more difficult to measure and to attribute to a specific intervention.

Graphic 7: Working With A "BIG BOX" Mission

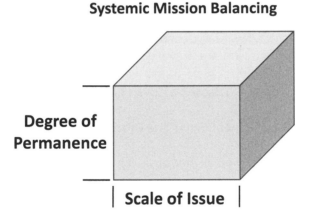

Systemic Mission Balancing

Degree of Permanence

Scale of Issue

Step Two: Fitting The Mission To The Organization

"Big Box" missions are frequently reserved for larger foundations. To fit or adjust the mission to a smaller foundation, the scope of work can be reduced without losing any power. One way to reduce the mission without abandoning the first-priority problem is to put a "collar" around the box to restrict activities. Collars can be geographic, conceptual, demographic or temporal but they all have the effect of narrowing the universe of possible activities.

A collar could be an important concept such as "democracy", a new approach such as "charter schools", a problem, disease, population of interest, or even a specific geography such as a city, region, or nation.

For instance, a grantmaker may choose to work on large-scale issues but only within the state of North Carolina. The range of possible challenges can be reduced to a more manageable assortment at the state border. This is an artificial collar to the extent that most problems do not respect contrived lines of separation such as the city limits or the political boundaries, but these divisions are convenient delimiters for a properly-scaled response.

Graphic 8: Creating A Collar Around The Mission

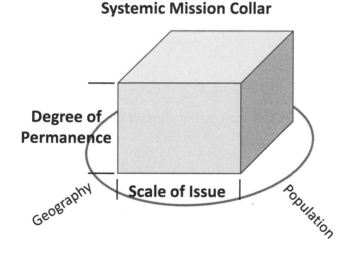

Another example of a common mission collar is selecting a certain population (i.e. all males) or a certain human condition (i.e. obesity). There are dozens of potential collars from among which to choose in order to achieve a tighter fit between the aspirations and assets of the funder.

A grantmaker may choose an even smaller box within which to work by using multiple collars at once. For instance, a grantmaker interested in a short-term, non-life-threatening challenge affecting a small number of people would clearly be working in a much smaller box and could write an appropriately scaled mission.

Graphic 9: Fitting The Mission To The Foundation

Reduced Mission Collar

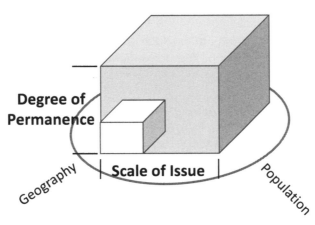

As an example of multiple collars, the elimination of unemployment is a very "big-box" challenge that can be reduced with a collar limiting the scope of work to a single city such as Charlotte. This could be followed with a second collar limiting the population of interest to first or second generation Vietnamese immigrants. With multiple collars, an overly expansive mission can be reduced to fit the size of the foundation. As a related benefit, a limited mission may also be more easily measured and achievable.

Another good example of the "small-box" mission would be to "save a World War II Sherman tank from deterioration so that it can be installed in a local history museum". The problem, left unattended, will result in irreversible damage to a very rare military artifact so the degree of permanent damage is high without quick intervention. But, the scale of the issue is small and the population effected by the effort is also small.

The benefits of a small-box mission include:
- The theory of change and the logic model are more easily understood.
- Progress can be more easily monitored and change happens quickly.

- Errors by the grantee or by the funder are not likely to be earth-shaking.
- The link between a grant and the end result is more obvious.
- A small-box mission is a proportionate fit for a foundation with a small endowment.

Whether a foundation chooses to work on a global scale, to tackle life-threatening challenges, with multi-generational implications, is also a function of the size of the funder's assets or of the collective assets of its partners. On one hand, it would be regrettable for a foundation with billions in its endowment to focus on small-box issues that could be confronted by several smaller organizations. Yet, it is far more common for smaller foundations to adopt grandiose missions that are difficult to measure.

Step Three: Writing the Mission

Many mission statements are written more like poetry than prose. Since many foundations commit a serious error in failing to define "What" they are trying to accomplish, it comes as no surprise that a poetic mission statement offers little navigational guidance after a little ornate language is added.

A funder with an overly poetic mission statement can take satisfaction in knowing that it is not likely to change for many years. They may also be satisfied that it is impossible to measure and may never be achieved. But, these statements lead to a lack of accountability because they offer almost no navigational help to the regulator, grantee, or general public. They have the benefit of being easily memorized for team-building or communication purposes and almost every grant can be considered a success.

Conversely, narrow mission statements that are very detailed and much easier to measure are also very limiting and may act to constrain the organization from taking advantage of dynamic events. Narrow missions can afford to be more technically oriented and can offer excellent navigational guidance to interested stakeholders, but these statements must be revised frequently. Too many adjustments to the mission may be viewed skeptically by both stakeholders and grantees; and, generate organizational fatigue as they enact parallel changes in just as quickly to stay in tune with the funder.

Mission Examples: Finding The Middle Ground

If an overly broad mission is difficult to measure, and an overly narrow mission is unnecessarily limiting, what remains? Finding the middle ground of a clear, flexible mission that is tightly associated with the desired outcome but broad enough to allow room to take advantage of changing conditions is the key. Finding the middle ground is more of an art than a science. The desired outcome of the founders or board of directors is usually the best place to start.

As another example, which is discussed in detail in Chapter Eleven, the desired outcome adopted by the fictitious "XYZ-Foundation" states:

> *"Ten years from now, all children in families living below the federal definition of poverty in Orleans Parish will: (1) have access to affordable health care and a medical home, (2) live in families with at least one adult with a stable source of employment, (3) live in a safe environment, free from threat and abuse, and (4) be regularly engaged in an age-appropriate social network with adult supervision."*

This is "What" the foundation imagines the result to be in ten years. Knowing the ten-year desired outcome, the board wrote a mission statement that framed its approach to grantmaking. The resulting mission statement is shown here to demonstrate how multiple collars can help define and limit the work of what would otherwise be an overly expansive view of the problem.

> *"The XYZ-Foundation will improve the physical, material, emotional, and social well-being of children in families living in poverty in New Orleans, Louisiana."*

This mission is still very broad but less so. Each major element in the body of the mission such as "physical" or "material" can serve as a launch-point for progressively more narrow definitions. The process of narrowing the mission down to very specific goals, objectives and action steps is covered in detail in Chapter Eleven. For now, it is sufficient to note that the mission should be revisited every few years or shortly following a major success or failure. A funder with a "big box" mission to confront a very complex and vexing problem is not likely to change the mission frequently even if it is revisited annually. A funder with a "small box" mission with precise definitions and measures will amend the mission more frequently.

The "What" family of decisions is inextricably linked to both the "Why" and "How" decisions, but, the "What" decision (i.e. the mission decision) is by far the most important. Without knowing *what* to do, a vision of success is impossible and any activity will succeed as well as any other. Like a ship without a rudder, navigation becomes impossible and, even worse, without a map navigation makes little difference in the outcome since any port will do. The "Why" question, explored next in Chapter Three, is essential to the development of a vision for the organization because it helps define and measure success. The "How" question is more about methodology and is discussed in detail in Chapter Four.

Key Points To Remember:

- The most important step in strategic philanthropy, and the one with the greatest effect, is the decision of "What To Do".

- Donors and foundations often jump off track because they do not adequately answer the question of "What" should be done, "Why" it should be done, and to create a vision of success.

- Creating a strong, clearly written mission question puts a wall around the foundation that: (1) helps applicants, grantees, and communities understand the focal point of the foundation, and (2) protects the foundation from mission-drift.

- Broad missions are like poetry; they sound nice but offer very little navigational help to the funder, community, grantee, or even the foundation itself.

- Contrary to prevailing wisdom, the mission is not permanent. Seriously revisit the mission statement every few years with a critical eye for clarity, adaptability, and appropriateness given changing circumstances.

- Small foundations frequently adopt overly broad missions with vast ambitions that are outsized compared to their endowment and capabilities.

CHAPTER THREE

Deciding "Why" To Do It

The second step in becoming a more effective philanthropist after answering the "What To Do" question is to answer the "Why Do It" question. The answer to the "Why" question helps explain the reasoning behind the mission statement and defines the image of success or the "vision" for the future against which progress can be measured. Some refer to this as the "theory of change" for the enterprise or the reasoning that links "What" is being done to "How" it is being done (21).

It is essential that the mission and the expected outcome be well understood very early in the process. The root cause of the problem, its magnitude, severity, and preventability should be well researched to confirm the necessity of the mission and to reinforce that something should be done to confront the issue.

The literature should contain evidence that the specific interventions and policies being considered are likely to succeed. Careful study should also identify the necessary conditions for success, potential collaborators, and community assets which can be leveraged by the foundation. The research required to answer adequately the "Why" question is obviously extensive and serves as the basis for the formation of an organizational vision of success which will be discussed later in this chapter.

Graphic 10: Preparation Makes All The Difference

Why Do It ?
Do your homework first!

Input & analysis

- Demographics
- Trends
- Community Needs
- Leadership Interviews
- Area Focus Groups   **MISSION**
- Projections
- Key Assets
- Target Populations

As an example of taking the time to do the necessary homework, imagine that a funder operating in a community notices that it has lost population for several years. Research discovers that field that offers the greatest opportunity to grow the population is "economic development". The funder now knows the "What To Do" answer is to "grow indigenous businesses and to recruit new enterprises from outside the region that produce a net gain in jobs and increase the average family income of the citizens". But, clarifying "Why" (because jobs have been leaving the area at an unacceptable rate) leads to the next question. If the funder works for ten year in the field of economic development how will it know it has been successful? Thus, at the outset, a vision of success is essential to link the "What" answer to the "How" answer.

The success of the foundation depends heavily on a clearly articulated vision. If the vision is well developed, the definition of success is incorporated into a measurable vision statement. Business schools often teach that a vision statement must also be dramatic and enduring, but *Supercharged Giving* contends that the effectiveness of a clear vision is often lost in those subsequent attempts to make it inspirational or immutable. Most of all, the vision must clearly define success in measurable terms. If the funder doesn't have a vision for its work, it can hardly be expected to know what success looks like.

Definition 3: Vision

> **A vision statement** is a description of what the organization intends to achieve in the future; the documented aspirations of the leadership by a specific date in the future without detailing the methods that will be used.

A clear, measurable vision for the future pulls the organization forward and helps drive its capacity and outputs to meet the future vision of success. The vision springs from the organization's understanding of "Why" it does its work.

The picture of "success" that inspires funders to donate more and for nonprofit grantees to work harder can be written narrowly or expansively and in the near future or the distant future. A near-term vision is normally focused on more easily attained operational measures and outputs.

Graphic 11: Near Term Vision Drives Production-type Results

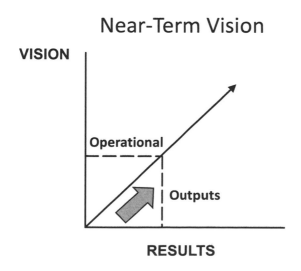

An example of a near term "operational" vision would be one that targeted the outputs of a production line or the number of teachers processed through a skills course. Many organizations in rapidly changing environments function with a near-term vision. As an example, a one-year near-term vision for a nonprofit organization that trains school leaders would be:

"By 2011 (*two years into the future*) the New Principal Development Program will train 42 teachers in preparation for advancement."

A three-year mid-term vision normally focuses on more substantive results and outcomes such as the one shown below.

"By 2015 (*five years into the future*) the New Principal Development Program will train 67 teachers in preparation for advancement **and place 27 graduates into principal or assistant principal positions.**"

Graphic 12: Stepped-Up Vision Focuses on Outcomes

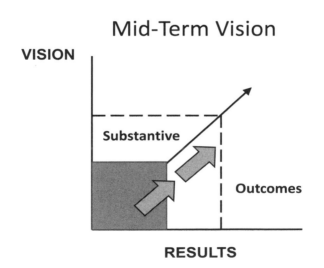

A five-year long-term vision normally focuses on significant, transformative change and impacts. For instance, the same principal development program with a long-term vision would focus the organization much differently.

"Vision- -By 2020 (*nine years into the future*) the New Principal Development Program will train 110 teachers in preparation for advancement, place 46 graduates into principal or assistant principal positions, and boost student achievement scores by 20% from 62.9 to 75.5 year-over-year in same-principal schools with 80% of all students graduating from NPDP schools going on to attend college."

The transformative nature of long-term, challenging visions can help boost the results from "outputs", to "outcomes", to "impacts". The real challenge over time for a funder is to stick to the work and the vision when the novelty has worn off and the anticipated results are still in the future. Long-term visions require patience and dedication to be fulfilled.

Graphic 13: Long-Term Vision Drives Impact

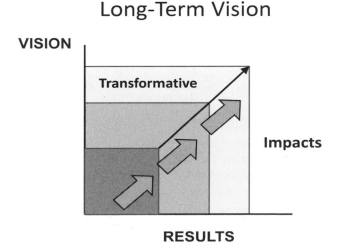

It is clear that the clarity and quality of the vision of an organization has a lot to do with its results. Stronger results, consequently, increase the size of the organization, improve its capacity to handle even more challenges, and develop durability in the face of set-backs. As a foundation strives to achieve its vision, its results are likely to improve over time. As its results improve, so does the demand for even more impact. As with most things, success breeds more success.

Foundations that produce great results also tend to attract attention from other funders. Other funders collaborate and he effect of the project is multiplied as more people work to achieve the original vision.

Graphic 14: Achieving the Vision Brings Growth

Vision Drives Results
Results Drive Growth

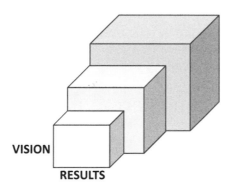

To summarize, if a funder can answer the "Why Do It" question, it probably has a clear vision of the road ahead. With a clear vision statement, the success of the foundation can be measured because it knows the desired outcomes of its work. Thus, with "success" defined, the vision for the organization is much easier to write and to communicate to others. While the vision is beyond immediate reach, if it is within the realm of possibility it should challenge the organization to produce transformative results.

Key Points To Remember:

- The answer to the "Why" question helps explain the reasoning behind the mission statement.

- Answers to the "Why" question help define what the board or the founder views as the ultimate measure of success of the grantmaking strategy at the enterprise level.

- Knowing the desired outcome of the grantmaking strategy leads directly to the "vision" of the organization or founder.

- A vision statement is a description of what the organization intends to achieve in the future; the documented aspirations of the leadership to be achieved within a certain time period without detailing the methods that will be used.

- The vision of the founder or of the board of directors drives the achievement of results and can be narrow and production-centered, or expansive and transformative.

- Over time, the vision and the subsequent attainment of desired results also tends to increase the size and operational capacity of an organization.

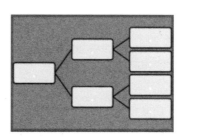

CHAPTER FOUR

Deciding "How" To Do It

The third major family of decisions is the "How" family. Strategies, theories of change, tactics, logic models, action steps, and budgets are all elements which provide a response to the "How To Do It" question. Generally, foundations and donors have proven better at achieving answers to the "How" question rather than to the "What" or "Why" questions. They are often deeply enmeshed in the process of grantmaking without having first determined what they are trying to do and why. As a result, they often adopt a very broad, difficult to measure mission to hide the fact that they do not really understand their ultimate objective. As discussed in Chapter Two, there are a few very large foundations with broad missions that are matched appropriately to their asset size. However, many small funders have adopted big, broad, missions and prove to be just ineffective dreamers (6; 17; 20).

Strategies, also known as "theories of change", have been widely accepted in philanthropy to help describe their reasoning behind a grant. As widely adopted as these terms are, half of the funders using the term "theories of change" do not understand what it means (17).

Definition 4: Strategy

Strategies are <u>theories of change</u> or the reasoning that describes the linkage between a given action and an outcome or why taking a certain action should produce a specifically desired result.

37

Graphic 15: The "What" And "How" Relationship

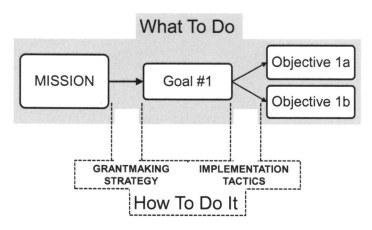

Graphic 16: Strategies Are "Theories of Change"

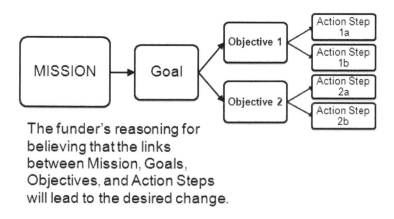

A goal is a derivative of the mission statement from which a more explicit description of what is to be done can be crafted. It can also be a useful container to create functional boundaries for a segment of grant-making work.

Definition 5: Goal

> **A goal** is an unambiguous statement of <u>what</u> should be done as a major measurable sub-set of the mission. If all goals are achieved, by definition, the mission has been accomplished.

It is difficult to imagine that the mission of a foundation can be fully accomplished by the attainment of just one goal. Most foundations create multiple goals to reflect each major segment of the mission.

Definition 6: Objective

> **An objective** is a very specific, unambiguous, measurable, time-limited statement of <u>what</u> should be done as a sub-set of a goal. If all objectives are achieved, by definition, the associated goal has been accomplished.

Graphic 17: Design With Multiple Goals and Objectives

Strategic Design

How does a grantmaker actualize an objective? Typically, they build a tactical plan that includes detailed action steps, and budgets often described collectively as "logic models".

Definition 7: Tactics

Tactics describe how a particular objective will be attained through the detailed sum of inputs, activities, and outputs (also known as a logic model).

Recall that objectives are in the "What" family of decisions and help define a larger goal. As a final element, each objective should have at least one detailed tactical step known as an "action step" which is accompanied by a specific budget of anticipated expenditures and a timeline.

Graphic 18: Logic Modeling & Tactics

Grantmaking Tactic As A Logic Model

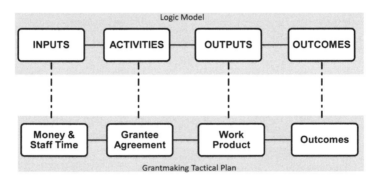

In theory, if all action steps have been completed, the associated objective has also been attained. Every action step supports and is connected to an objective.

If all action steps are achieved, by definition, the associated objective has been accomplished. Each action step is associated with a budget of anticipated costs for the next budget cycle (usually a fiscal year).

Definition 8: Action Step

> **An action step** is a very specific, unambiguous, measurable, time-limited statement of <u>what</u> should be done to accomplish an objective.

Graphic 19: Mission, Goals, Objectives & Action Steps

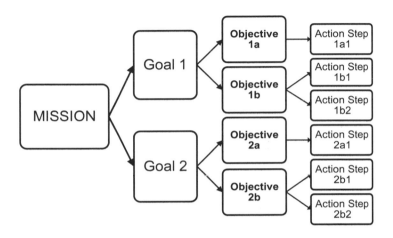

The resulting four-level strategic design produces a tightly connected series of elements in the "What" and "How" families with their associated strategic and tactical actions. A budget is connected to each action step and all budgets can be summed to equal a complete picture of the unit costs of achieving an objective.

There is nothing magical about using a strategic design to achieve the outcomes grantmakers desire. In fact, this process is commonly used by government, industry, and nonprofits. Most foundations don't use a similar process to guide their grant making. This is understandable because there is rarely a direct cause-and-effect relationship between a funded intervention and the observed outcome.

Graphic 20: Action Steps With Budgets

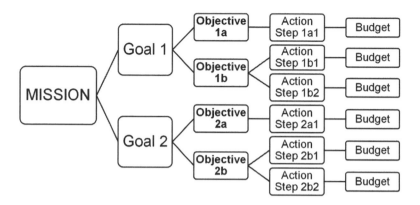

Thus, many funders prefer to avoid declaring their specific intentions at the beginning due to an inexplicable fear of failure, to dodge accountability, or because it is much more difficult to stay the course over time. It could be that they view philanthropic spending as requiring a less business-like approach which could account for a cavalier view of the money from a grantee perspective.

Image 2: Strategic Philanthropy Is Not A Magical Black Box

"We should clarify this part."

Key Points To Remember:

- Strategies, theories of change, tactics, logic models, action steps, and budgets fall within the "How" family of decisions.

- Strategies are the theories of change or the reasoning that describes the underlying assumptions of <u>how</u> the mission or a particular goal within the mission will be achieved.

- A goal is an unambiguous statement of <u>what</u> should be done as a major measurable sub-set of the mission.

- An objective is a very specific, unambiguous, measurable, time-limited statement of <u>what</u> should be done as a sub-set of a goal.

- Tactics describe <u>how</u> a particular objective will be attained through the detailed sum of inputs, activities, and outputs (also a logic model).

- An action step is a very specific, unambiguous, measurable, time-limited statement of <u>what</u> should be done as a sub-set of an objective

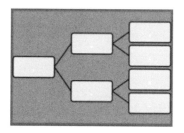

PART TWO

5. **Strategic Cycle;**
   Analysis & Input

6. **Strategic Design**

7. **Implement**

8. **Monitor**

9. **Evaluate & Adjust**

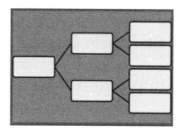

CHAPTER FIVE

Strategic Cycle
Phase I: Analysis & Input

The foundation's work doesn't end with the adoption of a clear mission statement and a vision of the desired grantmaking outcome. The funder should make strategic thinking part of its routine by adopting the five-phase planning cycle described here and in the following five chapters. Adopting a strategic cycle and using it year in and year out will imbed a systematic way of thinking strategically.

The strategic cycle starts with the regular review of the mission of the organization. The mission changes the least over time and should be a high-level, relatively durable statement of what the foundation is seeking to accomplish. It is tempting to gloss over the annual critique of the mission primarily because it is taken for granted that the mission doesn't change. However, as proposed in *Supercharged Giving*, the mission cannot be inflexible if the foundation has a perpetual life span. Perpetuity simply means the organization will last forever, not that its mission will never change. Additionally, since the mission will ultimately be achieved by definition, after all of the goals and objectives have been achieved, the mission should be forced into re-evaluation every few years. This approach establishes a cyclical, natural, expiration date usually within just a few years.

The lower-level, more specific elements of a plan are more variable the closer they are to short-term activities. Thus, goals change more frequently than the mission. Objectives change even more often and action steps are the most variable because they are nearest to the daily activities of the foundation staff. With the addition of budgets to the process, the entire planning cycle takes on a rhythm that follows the fiscal year of the organization. The cycle eventually becomes a permanent part of the life of the foundation.

Graphic 21: The Full Strategic Philanthropy Cycle

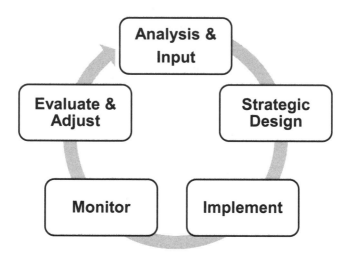

Strategic philanthropy involves a five-step sequential flow that does not end until the mission, as it is then stated, has been accomplished, renewed, or replaced. The cycle produces a reassessment of the entire grantmaking strategy before starting again with each new year.

Analysis & Input

The strategic cycle begins with the collection of information from the environment in which the funder operates. Next, the funder should analyze and sift through the information to fully understand the setting and conditions that are likely to influence the design of its goals. Finally, armed with a complete understanding of the challenges and opportunities, the funder can design a strategy to achieve the desired results. The analysis and input phase is one of the most overlooked and underrated phases in the strategic cycle. However, skipping this phase or drawing erroneous conclusions in haste contributes heavily to the subsequent failure of many grantmaking initiatives.

Graphic 22: The All-Critical Analysis Phase

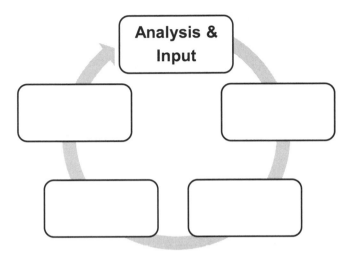

Careful and detailed analysis of the issues will either confirm the importance of the mission or force a reconsideration of the fundamental direction of the organization. If the mission is supported by thoughtful research, the desired outcome of the foundation's work is more understandable by stakeholders and staff. To get the most from this analysis, a review of the mission should be the first step in the process. In so doing, the mission and the desired outcome can be adjusted at little cost to the organization. This chapter reviews seven different elements that should be considered by funders before adopting or confirming the mission of the organization or before defining the vision of success.

1. Demographic Analysis

Demographic analysis of the target population is a must. Demographic analysis includes such variables as births, deaths, migration, and mortality, or distribution by age, race, or income. It can include the labor market and business composition and other elements of interest such as religion, gender, density, and even transportation and traffic studies.

For example, the population of interest can be identified by a single disease such as "diabetes", by affinity group such as "train lovers", or by geography such as the "citizens of New York". Regardless of the parameters (or "collars" from Chapter One), if the population of interest is known, a detailed working knowledge of its characteristics is an essential first step.

Findings can even be compared to other populations with similar characteristics for benchmarking purposes. Regardless of the details, a demographic analysis is a great place to start to understand the environment in which the funder works.

2. Trend Analysis

Trend analysis is the collection of information in an attempt to identify patterns over time. Historic trends help forecast or predict future events. Analysis of patterns can help establish a baseline against which change can be monitored. Depending on the specific variable, trends can help define the desired outcome(s) of an initiative by suggesting that a trend is good and should be reinforced or that a trend is unhealthy and should be altered. Trend analysis helps determine the relative effort that may be required to change the direction of a behavior and the scale of the investment that may be required from the funder.

3. Community Needs Assessment

A comprehensive community needs assessment is a critical element of strategic philanthropy and includes general community surveys, leader-interviews, focus groups, expert testimony, literature research, interventional modeling, and key asset analysis. Conducting a community needs assessment that focuses on a specific population also provides important information for developing a philanthropic strategy. Invariably, one or another need rises in its urgency or its domination of community functioning. A multiple-method needs analysis that examines and combines different types of data is a more complex approach but could also be more useful. The findings of a needs assessment can be used to help prioritize the issues confronting the target group and may even point the way to solutions that may be effective.

4. Leadership Interviews

Leadership interviews in the analysis phase of the cycle add the expert content that helps shape better diagnostics and may even help shed light on the likelihood of success of various potential interventional approaches. One-on-one interviews can add an element of confidentiality to deepen the findings. Likewise, a special leadership or key informant focus group can provide valuable input by developing interactive responses between the attendees that can be pursued by skillful moderators.

5. Focus Groups

Focus groups can be used to initiate open-ended discussions that may be representative of larger populations with similar characteristics as focus group members. A number of focus group designs are available depending on the type of information sought, such as two-way, dual, dueling, mini-focus group, respondent/moderator, client-participant, and others. Focus groups have been used in the social sciences and business to test products, analyze responses, identify problem issues, or to forecast larger group opinions.

6. Interventional Modeling

Interventional modeling is a technique that tests the social compatibility of a proposed program against the norms of a population. Some outcomes that are sought by funders can be modified, enhanced, or even abandoned on the basis of how the target population accepts the model. The usefulness of this technique in the analysis phase is optimal when the funder's desired outcome is directly or implicitly attached to a specific program design or methodology.

7. Key Asset Analysis

Key asset analysis places emphasis on the existing strengths (assets) and opportunities of a given population of interest rather than trying to overcome weaknesses or threats. The value of using an asset-based analysis of a given population of interest is that it tends to catalog and encourage the positive aspects of the group rather than dwelling on the negatives. This approach to environmental analysis is based on the principle of substitution in that no rational funder would pay to create assets that already exist in the community. Rather, funders build on existing assets as a way to strengthen the positive aspects of the target group.

Regardless of the methodology, the analysis and input part of the cycle is critical to later success. The analysis phase is time consuming and frustrating to funders or foundation executives who are ready for action but it pays big dividends by building an empirical base from which more effective decisions can be made.

Key Points To Remember:

- Properly designed mission statements have a natural expiration date that should challenge their applicability every few years.

- The mission changes the least over time but is not inflexible.

- Goals change more frequently than the mission. Objectives adapt even more quickly and action steps are the most highly variable.

- The entire strategic planning cycle should take on a rhythm that parallels the fiscal year of the organization.

- Understanding the environment in which a foundation or a donor functions is a basic premise for developing an effective mission, related goals, and strategies to achieve the mission.

- The strategic planning cycle has five phases including: analysis and input, strategic design, implementation, monitoring, evaluation and adjustment.

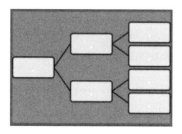

CHAPTER SIX

Phase II: Strategic Design

The next phase flows naturally from the new knowledge gained during the Analysis & input phase which produced an environmental assessment.

Graphic 23: Designing Strategies To Achieve The Mission

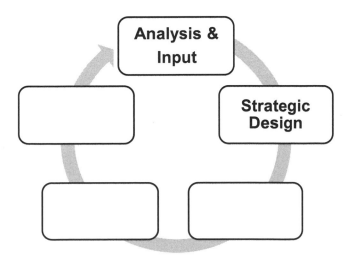

The choice of a strategic design is a product of two approaches: (1) an objective and systematic review of the literature, and (2) a subjective view of the environment. In this phase, the science and art of philanthropy coalesce. Objective analysis based on empirical evidence is combined with subjective opinions and viewpoints to form a blended product.

1. Research

To begin, funders should conduct an expert review of the literature associated with the desired outcome. This will produce a logical flow of ideas generated from current, relevant, and well-referenced sources. It should be an unbiased and comprehensive overview of the previous research related to interventions that may produce the desired outcome. Most communities have a nearby regional research university which may include specialists willing to conduct a literature review. There are also a wide range of commercial research institutions which may be capable of conducting a good literature review. Unfortunately, many literature reviews are not unbiased. College professors, like funders, have opinions and hold long-cherished viewpoints that can unwittingly point the funder in the wrong direction. One way to overcome this bias is to engage researchers from two philosophically divergent institutions.

As an example, assume that a funder has an interest in improving the academic achievement of public school students as the desired outcome of its mission. Asking for a literature review from a faculty member or graduate student in a traditional teacher's college may provide a range of traditional interventions such as enhanced tutoring, teacher skill-building, or system support. Such a literature review might not examine non-traditional approaches such as charter schools, vouchers, or home-schooling which could be obtained from another philosophically different university or research organization.

Once the funder is armed with a competently-done literature review of possible interventions targeting the desired outcome, the strategic design should be subjectively adjusted in light of the environment and donor preferences. Choosing a final strategic design or "theory of change" is heavily dependent on finding a workable balance between objective analysis of the various available interventions and the environment.

2. Literature Review

Before searching the literature, grantmakers should have a general question from which a research topic can be isolated as a result of the search. In many cases, a good way to start is with a well described community challenge such as: "Do school-based health clinics reduce student days lost to illness?"

Grantmakers must place a high degree of importance on conducting a thorough review of the literature to gain the most from strategic philanthropy and Concept Mapping (Chapter Eleven). The literature search helps identify relevant sources of information including books, journal articles, documents on the internet, and located in library holdings. Grantmakers can review research that has been conducted that is relevant to the chosen concepts and the underlying theories upon which the research was designed. They can get detailed definitions of variables for future comparability to their grant work and see what approaches succeeded or failed relative to their target population. A good literature review also identifies approaches that have failed and should not be attempted. These failed approaches can be included in a strategic plan as a reminder of "considered but rejected" ideas.

The purpose of a good literature review is NOT to identify and discuss every existing resource related to the chosen subject. It is to identify those approaches that are MOST RELEVANT to the proposed grant approaches. Careful judgment and experience tends to guide the selection of resources to include in a map and to exclude from a map.

The literature review also lets the grantmaker acquire sufficient depth in a particular discipline or issue to understand the key elements in a given field. This new understanding often educates the grantmaker on the wide range of possibilities in addressing a given community challenge.

Solutions to numerous community challenges confronted by grantmakers are found in the social sciences. The Social Sciences Citation Index (SSCI) is a great place to start a literature review when targeting a particular population for change. Another is the PsycINFO database that contains all the information from *Psychological Abstracts* which is a key secondary reference journal. ERIC (Educational Resources Information Center) is also a good source for a literature review focused on education.

Using the ERIC! database at http://www.eric.ed.gov/ " and the "Advanced Search button, the question is described into "term" search fields. Most literature reviews use one or two search fields (ERIC! allows up to three search fields). Using "Keywords" and limiting the search to journal articles, the first 10 "hits" are listed out of a possible 3,260. Since there is no single correct way to conduct the search, through a series of trial-and-error attempts using different terms, the list of relevant citations can be determined. Interesting articles can be copied and reviewed in detail and for closely related articles, an analysis of the bibliography may also yield several important citations.

Not all titles are equally relevant to the search. Scanning abstracts can help reduce the list of possibilities further. The reduced list can be shortened even more by repeatedly refined search terms. There may be important articles or books in the database under different search terms, so, varying terms and repeated searches can be helpful. Finally, different databases may also yield new resources so a search of SSCI and/or of PsycINFO may surface information buried in "health" instead of "education", etc.

A series of productive searches may produce a very relevant list of articles and books on the research topic. Good literature reviews, however, are not based on abstracts alone because abstracts do not contain sufficient detail about the theoretic rationale or the findings. Reading the full text of each article or book will add clarity on the question and help narrow the list of important information including the identification of ways to describe various elements and to measure outcomes in ways that may allow some comparability between studies.

Grouping similar themes or components learned from the literature review may produce the beginnings of a string of logic along the lines of natural clusters, divisions, or theories. However, not all clusters or factors are of equal importance to the grantmaker. As an example, a group of articles in a literature search on "school-based health clinics" imply a relationship between the presence of a clinic and local property values. While this cluster of references may be of passing interest, it may not be of fundamental importance to the grantmaker. As an example, real estate values may still show up in a strategic plan but only to demonstrate a theme that was identified and rejected.

After the current state of the field is known from the literature and from additional interviews with key thought leaders in the chosen field, a strategy can be designed that offers the greatest possibility of success.

Other stakeholders, such as community or civic leaders, may help in deciding the final strategic design based on their knowledge of the environment and the relative advantages or disadvantages of one approach over another. If other stakeholders have different ideas for the strategy, they should be invited to air those ideas at this stage in the process. This opportunity to provide input should not be intimidating or too time sensitive. For this reason, *Supercharged Giving* includes as an appendix a particularly successful process for gaining the input of groups and for reaching a prioritized ranking of suggested approaches.

Key Points To Remember:

- Designing the underlying strategy for a philanthropic plan relies on both objective and subjective information.

- A literature review of the science and applied interventions for the desired outcome of the funder's grantmaking is an essential first step in creating a plan.

- Not all literature searches are unbiased.

- Not all titles are of equal importance in a literature review. Titles should be selected that are closely related to the desired grantmaking outcome.

- After the current state of the field is known from the literature and from additional interviews with key thought leaders in the chosen field, a strategy can be designed that offers the greatest possibility of success.

CHAPTER SEVEN

Phase III: Implementation

The next element in the planning cycle is where the proverbial "rubber meets the road", the implementation of the chosen intervention.

Definition 9: Implementation

Implementation is a term used to describe the actualization or execution of a plan.

Four activities critical to the successful implementation of any grantmaking strategy are: (1) the allocation of donor resources, (2) the clarity of assignments, (3) the selection of the appropriate logic model, and (4) the identification of capable grantees.

Allocation Of Donor Resources

No funder has unlimited resources so they must decide how much of their limited grant money can be spent on each project being considered for implementation. Of necessity, some projects will be delayed while others go forward. The resource allocation decision is complicated whenever two or more competing goals and objectives exist in the same organization. This is not unusual but can be debilitating internally if not considered by the time that a project is implemented.

Graphic 24: Implementation, Working With Grantees

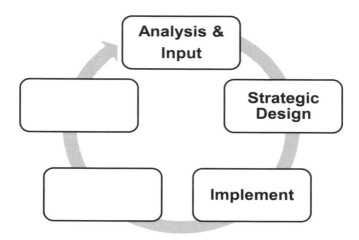

For instance, a foundation with a broadly stated mission to improve the health of the community could legitimately adopt several goals within the mission such as healthcare, employment, insurance, and housing among many others. Each goal is part of a carefully crafted grantmaking strategy that is clear, measurable, and cohesive, but, what goal takes priority and thus gets first call on resources?

In most foundations, resolving the tension between competing goals is poorly managed. While no widely accepted formulaic model exists to resolve the dilemma, prioritizing techniques can be used to take much of the pain out of reaching a consensus among key actors. Group dynamic tools such as "nominal group processes*" can help resolve conflicting prioritization decisions. Alternatively, goals can be rated as "high, medium, or low", reflecting their anticipated effect on the desired outcome. Still another approach to prioritization would be to use a "maximizing matrix" that balances outcomes, cost, and time. Regardless of the approach, prioritization of grantmaking goals is unavoidable and critical to the successful implementation of a grant-supported project.

*A full description and example is included as an appendix to *Supercharged Giving* as a book bonus.

Implementation Logic Model

Constructing the right logic model to support the implementation of a grant-supported project involves inputs, activities, outputs, and outcomes. It is the right combination of money, staff time, management of process through the grantee agreement, the work product, and the outcomes of the project.

Graphic 25: Grantmaking Logic Model

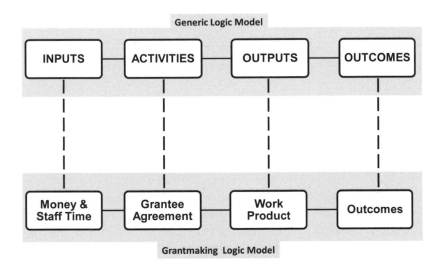

Experienced grantmakers use the logic model to build the basics of an operating budget for implementation. The "inputs" cover many more topics than money and staff including rent, utilities, travel, consulting expertise, etc. The grantee agreement is critical to implementation because it spells out the cash flow, timelines, reports, data collection methods, evaluation plan, and anticipated work product. The outputs are often service-oriented frequencies such as the number of teachers trained, nurses graduated, or new jobs created from other sources. The outcomes are the result of the work product such as increased student performance scores, reduced emergency room visits, etc. The development of the logic model for implementation can be complex and could be completed in two steps. The first step takes the model to the limit of the literature search (Chapter Six) and the second step fills in more of the specific details after the grantee has been selected and can participate in the design.

The grantmaking logic model is a detailed plan for achieving an objective. Since the environment and the grantee are very dynamic and constantly changing, many foundations implement an objective "on the fly". Supercharged Giving recognizes the volatile nature of the implementation phase but proposes that they can be much more effective if they approach the implementation phase with as much respect as they do the strategic design phase. While implementation is fraught with changing conditions and hazards that threaten the achievement of the overall objective, using a flexible logic model produces better results than an undisciplined "do it now" approach.

Clarity of Assignments

Role definition and separation can give a line of clear delineation between the purpose of the board of directors, the founder, or major donors and the responsibilities of the chief executive, management, and program officers resulting in a more effective dynamic between the two groups as an ultimate benefit to the community (31).

A frequent foundation error in implementing a strategic plan is in violating the functional roles of the key actors (4). The funder or the foundation board should limit its activities to governing. The role of the board of directors is primarily to maintain accountability, good governance, organizational conduct, and to measure and monitor effectiveness. The board is also responsible for avoiding overly restrictive bureaucracy and inflexibility through honest feedback systems with the community and grantees. Occasionally, members of the board of directors or the founder start acting like program officers inappropriately dictating rules and suggesting operational details.

On the other hand, sometimes management starts acting like the board by making policy decisions that should be solely within the purview of the board or founder. The role of the management and staff is primarily as technical experts that link the board policy and mission to the actions of the foundation. This role confusion is common among nonprofits in general but it is particularly observable among foundations.

Graphic 26: Role Confusion

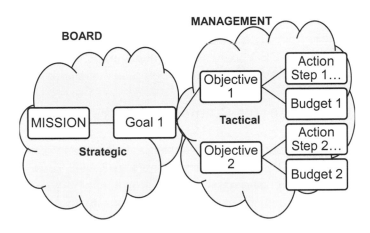

Confusion can also stem from unwillingness on the part of foundations or nonprofits to apply corporate discipline to enforce operating principles that have long been adopted by business. Regardless, role confusion between management and the board impedes success in many philanthropic organizations (31). While some wrongly believe that the work of a funder is easy (anyone can give away money, right?), this is not a view held by serious donors. The "easy" attitude can add to role confusion by treating the work too casually. Investing in effective nonprofits in order to create important social change is often a complex undertaking.

In this regard, rather than arguing over who is in charge, a key element distinguishing effective philanthropy from ineffective philanthropy depends on maintaining focus on the objectives of the organization (32). While the board, founder, or major donor may bring passion to the discussion, they rarely bring operational expertise in a given grantmaking discipline or social specialty.

Another issue can arise from the role of the chief executive as a voting member of the board. Supercharged Giving suggests the role of management and the role of the board or founder should be kept separate to protect the independence of each. This conceptual distinction still rages in corporate America between the chief executive's role and the board chairman's role (31). Among nonprofits in general and foundations in specific the preponderance of practice is to keep the two separate.

When the CEO is also a voting member of the board of a foundation, there is also a likelihood of a family connection to the donor or a key transition role from such as often exists in health legacy foundations. Where such dual CEO/board appointments exist in foundations, it is likely that role confusion is a significant drag on overall performance.

Selection of Capable Grantees

Of fundamental importance in the implementation phase of a foundation project is the selection of capable grantee(s) essential to performing the work outlined in the strategic plan. The grantee brings organization, skills, additional funding, staff, and experience to the implementation phase of a foundation's strategic process.

The grantee selection process is an important function of the foundation because it identifies the best qualified charities, signals other funders to watch and support the best charities, holds grantees accountable for transparency, and helps advance the effectiveness of the field by eliminating poor performers (14).

The relationship between grantees and foundations is almost always one of a power imbalance. Funders bring ideas, money, and staff expertise to the relationship but often with a "take it or leave it" attitude which is not particularly endearing to grantees. Many foundation leaders rely on the "golden rule" (he who has the gold, sets the rules) to keep grantees performing and coming back, often regardless of the true relationship below the surface. It is unfortunate that truly collaborative and consultative relationships between grantees and foundations are infrequent.

A positive relationship between grantees and funders can enhance grantmaking effectiveness substantially. Grantees and funders need each other. The relationship is symbiotic in that it each party needs the other in order to accomplish their goals. The relationship is so essential, that many foundations now turn to grantees to help evaluate the effectiveness of the foundation (3; 30).

Key Points To Remember:

- Implementation is a term used to describe the actualization or execution of a plan.

- Funders must decide how much of their limited grant money can be spent on each project being considered for implementation. In most foundations, resolving the tension between competing goals is poorly managed.

- Constructing the right logic model to support the implementation of a grant-supported project involves inputs, activities, outputs, and outcomes.

- A frequent foundation error in implementing a strategic plan is in violating the functional roles of the key actors.

- The grantee selection process is an important function of the foundation because it identifies the best qualified charities, signals other funders to watch and support the best charities, holds grantees accountable for transparency, and helps advance the effectiveness of the field by eliminating poor performers

- It is difficult to terminate a poor performing grant program but without simple goals, objectives, strategies, and tactics, even finding a poor performing program is hard.

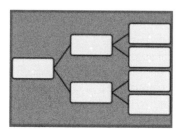

CHAPTER EIGHT

Phase Four: Monitor Progress & Results

The fourth phase of the annual strategic process is monitoring progress during the implementation and on-going operation of a project.

Definition 10: Monitoring

Monitoring is the systematic observation of the progress of an on-going operation or activity measured against previously established goals using indicators and benchmarking techniques as a routine management tool.

The monitoring function is broad-based as it interacts across a wide spectrum of the strategic cycle from the mission to individual action steps and budgeting. Properly done, every level of the "what to do" family of decisions includes an indicator that can be used to measure progress and a monitoring element is present.

Monitoring allows management to observe progress before errors or variances from norms or standards cause serious damage or even stop the program. It provides useful feedback about a dynamic process in time to make corrections. Even in situations in which a funded project shows no impact, monitoring may help identify the point and the processes that failed to deliver as expected (33).

Graphic 27: Monitoring Step

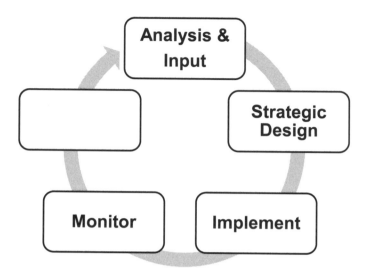

Funders often require grantees to produce quarterly reports that include monitoring information for financial and operational aspects of a funded program. The indicators used in a monitoring program may also evolve into institutionalized feedback that constantly allows adjustments to reach or maintain high-performance. As a result, funders often structure the quarterly report to serve as a management tool for the duration of the grant and to benefit the grantee as an operational tool.

Selecting Indicators

An indicator is a measure of change or status in a specific variable that facilitates tracking and understanding that variable. For instance, "degrees in Fahrenheit" are simple measures of temperature. However, when associated with water, the measure becomes an *indicator* that facilitates tracking change in water from a solid state (freezing) to a vapor (boiling). The selection of an appropriate indicator for any given variable can be very difficult in the social sciences. As an example, is "child health" best measured using "infant mortality", "child immunization rates", or "quality of life scores"? The best answer depends on the nature of the intervention being studied and the special nature of the population of interest.

Indicators can include process measures of activity, outcome measures of results, or even impact measures of the consequences of implementing the intervention. Variables and indicators that define and measure change in more specific ways are typically associated with lower-level goals and objectives. Variables and indicators tied to each action step can be monitored in even more precise terms at more closely spaced intervals.

At the highest level of the "mission", the work of the organization is associated with an equally high-level indicator which is probably slow to change. It is also likely that it will be difficult to find a strong correlation between the chosen indicator and the affect of any particular funded project and almost impossible to show causality. Even with these difficulties, *Supercharged Giving* is biased in favor of trying to measure and monitor the outcomes and impacts of most funded programs for the sake of learning what works and what doesn't and to help hold grantees accountable within reason.

Data Collection

A key requirement of proper monitoring is the collection of the appropriate data. Data collection is likely to occur an annual basis for "mission-level" indicators and may come from original data (such as a random survey of a population) or from secondary data (such as a standardized survey that is routinely given to all fourth grade students in the state or region). Progress is slow at the mission level of the organization, but progress can be measured and the findings may be useful in learning if a particular intervention or activity produces the desired effect. If the specific indicator is collected in other nearby states or regions, comparative benchmarking can be an added benefit.

Goals are subsidiary to the mission but they are directly connected depending on the purpose and wording of the mission. Goals are more likely to be associated with more specific, narrowly defined, indicators than the mission and data may be simpler and easier to collect, analyze and track. Objectives are even more specific and often relate most closely to the outcomes of a particular interventional program or grant with an associated indicator. As the level of the guiding statement declines from mission to goal and then to objectives and action plans, the indicator associated with each level is also more narrowly targeted.

Graphic 28: Points of Structural Measurement

Measurement

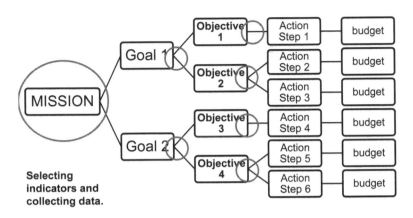

Monitoring

After identifying appropriate indicators and establishing data collection procedures, funders and grantees can monitor their mutual progress in achieving the goals and objectives of the project. Monitoring is a management tool for mid-course corrections after a project is started. Selecting indicators that directly or indirectly measure changes in the community in relation to the mission, goals, or objectives of the funder is an important part of creating a routine monitoring approach.

A few monitoring methodologies for foundations have surfaced in recent years including the balanced scorecard (34) or the multi-dimensional assessments (35) in addition to the performance pacing approach described in following chapters. All of these approaches have in common the use of perception-driven instruments.

Some approaches measure internal viewpoints, some include external examiners, some use grantee-based instruments, but all approaches are attempts to overcome the inherent weakness of a uniformly applicable metric for measuring foundation performance.

Graphic 29: Board and Management Monitoring Tools

Monitor

–Monitoring System:

Dashboard, Report Cards, Success Score, Watch, Grantee Satisfaction Survey, Community Indicators

–Enforce Compliance

–Pay Attention to Variances

Key Points To Remember:

- Monitoring is the systematic observation of the progress of an on-going operation or activity measured against previously established goals using indicators and benchmarking techniques as routine management tools.

- An indicator is a measure of change or status in a specific variable that facilitates tracking and understanding that variable.

- Selecting indicators that directly or indirectly measure changes in the community in relation to the mission, a goal, or an objective is crucial to effective monitoring.

- Funders often require grantees to produce quarterly reports that include monitoring information for financial and operational aspects of a funded program.

- The indicators used in a monitoring program may also evolve into institutionalized feedback in the grantee's organization that constantly allows for adjustments to reach or maintain high-performance.

CHAPTER NINE

Phase Five: Evaluate & Adjust

The fifth phase of the annual strategic cycle includes an evaluation of the activities of the grantees and of program results across the entire family of "what to do" decisions from the general mission to specific objectives. The difference between the monitoring phase and the evaluation phase is subtle. Evaluation about the ultimate effectiveness of programs or new theories of intervention, providing input about program funding, design, or administration. Monitoring is about the progress being made toward a specific goal and is a management tool to make mid-course adjustments.

Funders should identify the desired outcome of a program or grantee activity sufficiently to select the type of evaluation that will be most useful for the grantee and the foundation. Knowing the purpose of the evaluation will help the grantee and evaluator design an efficient and specific evaluation approach including selecting variables and indicators, data collection, a plan of analysis, and identification of important viewpoints.

In order of importance, the five primary functions of evaluation are discussed below.

1. Learning--educating the grantee and the funder about what is and is not effective about a supported program is the most important function of evaluation. Evaluation provides direction for refining the program model or modifying how the program has been implemented. It also instructs the funder. Evaluation can show how effective the funder is being at the macro level of the whole enterprise. It can also isolate a cluster of grants to show how several projects are acting in concert. Most commonly, evaluation can measure the success or failure of a single grantee or project against the desired outcome. Learning from evaluation supports the strategic planning process and serves as a basis to monitor the state of the literature in all operational disciplines. Evaluation is also very instructive to program officers by keeping them up on advances in the field.

Graphic 30: Full Strategic Cycle

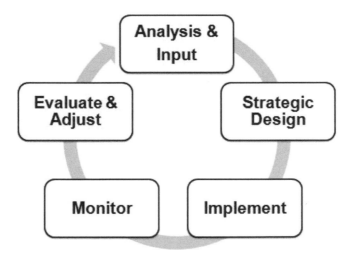

2. Accountability--showing the activities, outputs, and outcomes grantees actually achieve on a routine basis serves to hold grantees and the funder accountable for results.

3. Sustainability--demonstrating in an objective way the benefits of a program helps the grantee advocate its benefits to other funders, agencies, and companies thus helping to sustain good programs.

4. Cost-efficiency & effectiveness--identifying outcomes that the program delivers per dollar expended (efficiency) can be compared to alternative programs with the same or similar outcomes to allow more in-formed decisions by the funder about re-investing in or disseminating information about the program or grantee (effectiveness).

5. Dissemination--showing others the benefits of the program draws attention and helps change public opinion in favor of grantees with suc-cessful models.

There are many types of evaluation including formative, process, sum-mative, outcome, and impact models. The type of evaluation that is ap-propriate for a particular intervention depends to a great extent on the context and purpose. If the intent is process improvement, a formative or process evaluation is best. If the intent is accountability, a summative evaluation might do the job. Knowledge generation evaluations are usu-ally for broader audiences and advocacy and the intervention itself may even be secondary to the need for precise measurement of a particular theory such as when supporting a new or novel intervention with regional or national implications. The stage of the program being evaluated, the political context of the program, and the structure of the program also influence the design of the evaluation.

Definition 11: Evaluation

Evaluation is the use of research procedures to systematically investi-gate the effectiveness of grant-supported programs from identification of the problem to conceptualization and model design, program imple-mentation, outcomes, and impact.

Foundations will find it easier to identify the nature and resources to de-vote to an evaluation when they have determined all of the "what" and "how" decisions in advance. Well designed approaches to grantmaking find a good evaluation program to be the source of strategic feedback and institutional learning.

Establishing Evaluation Policy

Funders keen on learning from their grants and grantees spend consid-erable time and valuable resources on evaluation. Foundation boards and key officers often find themselves engaged in the arcane details of evaluation conceptualization and design, data collection, variables, indicators, etc. Without sufficient professional training in research methodology and experience in program evaluation, too much time spent at the policy level can be distracting and should be avoided.

In order to focus on important strategic issues and also gain the considerable intelligence that can come from evaluation, funders should consider adopting an evaluation philosophy and policy. With this policy as guidance, the policy-level demands are reduced to exceptions rather than going through the discussion as each funding decision is made. A sample evaluation policy and grant classification schema can be found at www.philoptima.org.

Evaluators & Program Officers

Program officers and evaluators view the world differently. As a result, a natural tension exists between them. They vie for control and influence in a world constrained by limited resources and defined by powerful relationships. They are rarely completely comfortable with each other for good reason; too much familiarity could imperil the work, strategy, and effectiveness of the foundation.

Program officers initiate and oversee the implementation of grant programs for funders. They work to overcome some of the most vexing challenges facing society and they do so with limited grant budgets, undercapitalized nonprofit partners, and restricted help from the home office. They are in the field and develop deeply held passions and lasting relationships with their fellow soldiers in the war against poverty, injustice, ignorance, (choose the fight). Program officers are the official "face" of the foundation among one of the most important publics to funders: nonprofit organizations.

Program officers are stretched thin most of the time. They have too many grants to manage and too few hours in the day. However, in their rush from one project, alliance, collaboration, or meeting to the next, they develop a heightened ability to identify a pure opportunist or a passionate purist. At the end of the day, they can often be found at home, bent over the kitchen table, filling out that final report demanded by their employer that can spell life or death for their nonprofit partner.

Evaluators are trained in the scientific approach and rarely establish deeply held or passionate convictions about programs or people funded by foundations. They are bright and energetic; dispassionate, and objective. Evaluators are not anti-social, but they should maintain some emotional distance from program officers because they are trained and employed to cast a critical eye on projects funded by their employer. They are the natural antagonists of program officers. For the very reason that program officers should not establish too comfortable of a relationship with their nonprofit partners, the evaluator must also maintain objectivity and clarity.

At best, the relationship between program officers and evaluators is cooperative but cool. At worst, the relationship can be tense or even acrimonious. The tension can divide and antagonize everyone involved in the organization from the front desk receptionist to the board member and the community leader.

To function effectively, employees in these two positions need "rules of engagement" that serve to keep natural differences at bay and bring out the strengths of both. Foundations hoping for relatively peaceful relationships should establish the rules in such a way as to avoid giving either viewpoint an overwhelming advantage. As an example, a foundation can focus primary responsibility for its relationship with grantees on program officers rather than evaluators. The foundation thus avoids establishing multiple authoritative points of contact with the same grantee so that essentially all communication with grantees flows through one person. This approach minimizes the potential for miscommunication and improves accountability because there is no one else to blame for bad results.

Channeling all communications with grantees through a program officer can be a disadvantage to the evaluator because it is the evaluator who is charged with the responsibility of passing judgment on the success or failure of a grant program in the field and for data collection, observation, and monitoring. Thus, much of an evaluator's success rests on maintaining positive relationships with program officers who, in turn, rely on their relationships with grantees. From the viewpoint of the foundation, the program officer is armed with some natural advantages that evaluators do not have. Program officers are the external "face" of the foundation to the community and grantees. They hold the key to relationships with grantees and thus greatly influence the overall success of the foundation. Evaluators are more frequently internally focused and are less directly connected to grantees while remaining attentive to outcomes.

To counter-balance these natural advantages of the program officer, foundations often implement a policy that segments the evaluation function by grant size or anticipated impact. Small grants are evaluated by the program officer in combination with the nonprofit grantee. Large grants, on the other hand, are evaluated by independent, skilled, external evaluators answering to the foundation's internal evaluator after having been selected by joint agreement between the grantee, program officer, and evaluator.

While the program officer has the power advantage in the field, the evaluator often has the power advantage in the board room. When called upon to report on the findings of a formal evaluation, regardless of the type, the evaluator's opinion and conclusions are critical to most future funding decisions about the program. To this end, the evaluator's opinion should not even be suppressed by upper management with a differing position. Thus, some evaluators are granted a special protected status to report findings directly to the board or the board chair.

Evaluation is at the heart of understanding; programming is at the heart of doing. Good evaluators are invaluable to any foundation or funder because they are somewhat like a "whistle-blower". They disrupt the otherwise comfortable relationship that often exists between grantees and program officers. Establishing a workable balance between these often competing roles is a real test of skill for the chief executive officer (CEO), founder, or board member. Both functions are critical to the long term success of the foundation and both should be welcomed and nurtured. The CEO may occasionally be called upon to extinguish the flames, but keeping a positive working relationship between program officers, grantees, and evaluators is worth the effort and the heat.

Self-Evaluation

There is little evidence that foundations have abused the many freedoms they enjoy, but they are widely accused of being secretive, even pompous and whimsical, in their grantmaking. Assuming there is some truth to these accusations, funders and foundations are increasingly at risk of ever more intrusive regulation unless they adopt more transparent and effective practices (36). In spite of this vulnerability, few foundations go out of their way to obtain independent reviews of their procedures and grantmaking (37).

The founders or board members are uniquely positioned to demand a culture of organizational self-appraisal in order to enliven public account-ability. A self-evaluation is not focused on grantees or funded programs. Instead, a self-evaluation attempts to systematically explore the function-ing of the foundation or funder's organization using various tools and viewpoints.

Funders will consider several principles when addressing the issue of accountability and self-evaluation. For starters, foundations should adopt a planning process that engages, in a substantial way, the per-spective and expertise of grantees and community advocates. They should jealously guard the nonprofit mission of the organization and avoid conflicts of interest and self-dealing. The founder or board will also encourage independent thought and seek expertise in the disciplines in which it works.

Graphic 31: Evaluating the Funder

Evaluating the Funder
- Evaluation of Board Functionality
- Monitoring Attendance Rules
- Analysis of Proxies & Voting Practices
- Confirming Residency Requirements
- Assessing Committee Functionality
- Auditing Bylaw Compliance
- Applying Conflicts of Interest Rules
- Tracking Grantee/Community Views

Further, the board should establish a culture which actively seeks com-munity input and ongoing, meaningful community involvement. Self-evaluations based on these principles help reinforce reflective behaviors and enhance foundation effectiveness.

Evaluating Board Functionality

An important aspect of a well-rounded self-evaluation process is assessing the functionality of the board of directors through a confidential survey instrument. Survey participants typically include board members but may also include important organizational actors. The survey should include questions about the organization of the board, the role of every committee, the level of engagement between operational and policy-level issues, the timeliness and adequacy of reading material that informs board members of meeting agenda items, management of the board meetings, composition of the board, relationship to the chief executive, length of board meetings, control systems such as the accounting and spending policies, etc. Questions should be a mix of open -ended and multiple choice items.

The survey should be delivered with a return envelope directed to the chair of the board at his/her home of place of work but not back to the foundation. All completed surveys should be reviewed first by the chair to screen confidential comments and then second by the chief executive for data assembly and report preparation. Finally, the results should be used to guide an in-depth confidential discussion in moderated by the chair or a disinterested external facilitator.

Monitoring Attendance Rules

It is a good-governance practice for boards to adopt attendance rules that encourage the physical presence of members at meetings of the board and each committee to which members are assigned. Lax attendance enforcement leads to lower levels of engagement and interest. Attendance should be carefully monitored and reported to all members in an open forum such as through a schedule attached to every board meeting agenda. Some foundations have adopted rules that automatically expel board members who fail to meet minimum attendance requirements.

Telephone and other electronic means of attendance should be acceptable in a few defined instances and on a limited number of occasions. A disengaged board member or family member of the founder is a leading indicator of governance failure. The ability of the chair or founder to "excuse" an absence should be confined to special circumstances such as illness or out-of-state travel and, even then, be limited to no more than 10-25% of all meetings. A good board self-evaluation should report all attendance variations for each member over a specified time (such as once each year at the annual meeting).

Analysis of Proxies & Voting Practices

If proxies are permitted for board or family foundation voting, they should be designated only between fellow board members. A proxy should always be time or event specific and limited as to authority. Many boards allow the abuse of proxies by permitting them to be assigned to non-board members such as the chief executive. This is an inappropriate use of the proxy because the CEO does not have the ultimate fiduciary responsibility for the organization like a member of the board. A proxy should only be given from one board member to another. Proxies should always be filed in advance of the meeting with the chair or otherwise be considered invalid.

To avoid internal lobbying of one board member by another and to limit the dominance of board meetings by members with strong personalities, some boards require secret ballots to approve all major expenditures or to approve a grant. Balloting can be accomplished quickly in such instances by using any one of several modern electronic voting systems.

An annual self-evaluation should also include an analysis of the use of proxies and voting practices compared to policy standards adopted by the board. Such an analysis may indicate a need to tighten practices that have evolved into lax patterns.

Confirming Residency Requirements

Many foundations require that board members live in the communities or states served by the organization. A residency requirement assumes that board members will have a better feel for community needs than persons not living in the region. When a board requires a certain residency status, the actual residency of each member should be confirmed as part of a self-assessment. Similarly, the organization may restrict board membership to people with certain religious, gender, or age conditions. If so, a self-assessment should surface any variations from policy and those variations should be reported to the chair and to the governance committee or board.

Assessing Committee Functionality

In the same fashion as the board conducts an assessment of its functionality, each committee should solicit and collect similar input from its membership.

Auditing Bylaw Compliance

A complete self-assessment should include a review of the articles of incorporation and the bylaws to identify all mandatory practices to which the board should adhere. A comparative review of actual practices should reveal any important variations that should be addressed by modifying behaviors.

Applying Conflicts of Interest Rules

The board's conflict of interest policy should establish the standard for internal and external conflicts and for the resolution of those conflicts when they occur. Board members and key officers should complete a conflict of interest survey as part of the self-assessment. Sensitive matters raised by the members should always be resolved by the chair to the benefit of the organization. All conflict surveys should be reviewed by the chair and any variances to the policy should be reported to the board and resolved without delay.

Tracking Grantee/Community Views

A self-evaluation is incomplete without the confidential input of grantees and community members. Confidentiality is critical because most grantees are reluctant to threaten their relationship with a key funding source by proffering honest criticism. There are numerous ways to collect this information, but if grantee perceptions are tracked consistently over several years, the foundation may discover issues that grantees are unwilling to raise in more open forums. Larger community views can be solicited through internet-based survey instruments or random mail or telephone surveys conducted under strict confidentiality by external consultants or polling specialists.

Adjust & Repeat

At the end of the annual strategic cycle, the foundation's strategic plan may look very different from its initial design. Throughout the year, circumstances change as the plan is implemented. The first things to change are often the action steps or budgets of a grant or initiative. The speed of accomplishment of one tactical step in the plan may hold another step back thus delaying progress on an entire objective. Part way through the year, it is possible that one objective became unattainable for any of a million reasons. The plan should be adjusted when insurmountable barriers are encountered. As plans are adjusted, some lines of activity may be abandoned and the resources in the plan can be redistributed in favor of other opportunities in the plan that may be successful.

Throughout the year, the realities brought on by attempting to implement the strategic philanthropic plan may require adjustments. Rarely does the mission need to be amended in just one yearly cycle, but, even the mission may need to be adjusted in light of changed conditions such as a natural disaster in the region, the departure of a major business, or the sudden influx of a new population. A lesser goal may continue to be important, but the objectives that derive from the goal may need adjustment in light of new information. The most volatile changes to the plan occur when one or more of the action plans need to be adjusted but these are also the easiest to adapt to new circumstances.

Being prepared and willing to change when necessary is just part of the process. Change, however, should involve the parties closest to a particular layer in the plan. For instance, the board should be involved and approve changes to the mission, and to the "what" and "how" decisions. Lower level adaptations should engage appropriate levels of management and perhaps even grantees. Program officers and the accounting department should be involved in changing tactics such as action steps and budgets so long as these modifications are governed by board-approved spending policies.

The annual philanthropic plan should also be critiqued by a few trusted grantees and an external evaluator or analyst. A system of periodic listening and feedback will also help guide the development of the plan. Examples of external feedback include grantee satisfaction surveys, site visits, financial audits, or internal process critiques by experienced practicing philanthropists. It is difficult to terminate a poor-performing grant, but without simple goals, objectives, strategies, and tactics, even finding a poor-performing grant can be a challenge. Finally, changes in the environment or among grantees or within the staff create new opportunities that will require new resources. Revisiting and refreshing the strategic plan once or twice during the year provides an opportunity to challenge and test the assumptions upon which it was designed and adopted before the fiscal year started.

Key Points To Remember:

- Evaluation is at the heart of understanding; programming is at the heart of doing.

- Evaluation is the use of research procedures to systematically investigate the effectiveness of grant-supported programs from identification of the problem to conceptualization, model design, program implementation, outcomes, and impact.

- In order to focus on important strategic issues and also gain the considerable intelligence that can come from evaluation, funders should consider adopting a written evaluation philosophy and policy.

- The founders or board members are uniquely positioned to demand a culture of organizational self-appraisal.

- It is difficult to terminate a poor-performing grant but without simple goals, objectives, strategies, and tactics, even finding a poor-performing grant can be impossible.

- An important part of a well-rounded self-evaluation process is assessing the functionality of the board of directors through a confidential survey instrument.

- At the end of the annual strategic cycle, the foundation's strategic plan may look very different from its initial design

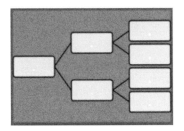

PART THREE

10. Grantmaking Processes, Products & Styles

11. Concept Mapping

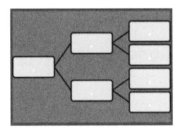

CHAPTER TEN

Grantmaking Processes, Products & Styles

Bumping Against Limitations

As the size of a foundation increases, it tends to act more like a business and adopt more sophisticated processes (18; 38). It also divides the labor into more specialized workers and decentralizes decision making (39). Coincidentally, as foundations increase in size, they decrease in effectiveness (*ibid.*). This falling performance may be caused by a mismatch between how the foundation is organized and the environment in which it operates. It may also be suffering from a disconnect between its grantmaking style and grantmaking products. In any event, too much money in a foundation can produce its own problems and limitations.

In the external environment, another major limitation is the capacity of the nonprofit community to perform effectively. Funders rely heavily on nonprofits to get the work done and a weak group of grantees will almost surely cast a long shadow back to the foundation. Once again, money is not everything. The contingency theory of organization suggests that the most effective organizations are more closely attuned to environmental conditions (40). In other words, a funder's grantmaking processes, grant products, and styles should closely match the design of the organization and the capacity of its grantee community in order to reach the highest levels of performance.

A Wide Range of Processes

Grantmakers use a wide range of bureaucratic grantmaking processes to handle their spending. Some contend that the

processing bureaucracy merely adds a patina of legitimacy to the decisions made by foundations, creating the appearance of being well managed without actually being so (4; 13). Historically, however, the development of a certain depth of bureaucracy in almost any form or organization fosters a higher level of performance (41; 42). It appears that some foundations, and perhaps most notably many large foundations, place more emphasis on their rules and processes than on the decision itself (11).

Graphic 32: Contingency Theory of Performance

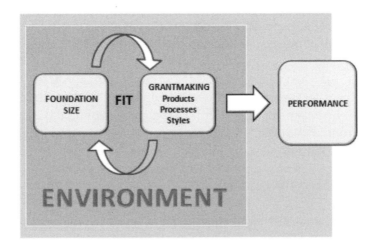

A certain level of processing must occur in order for the foundation to function. The debatable point is when to develop a processing bureaucratic system and when to avoid doing so. Research indicates an inverse relationship exists between bureaucracy and size which means that performance falls as more bureaucratic systems are installed (18). This noted, some processing must occur to implement the directives of the founder, board of directors, or donor. Additionally, how a grant is processed will differ with the type of grant and style of grantor. The most frequent grant processing systems include: strategic, transom, request for proposals, discretionary, directed, and uniform.

Strategic Systems

Strategic grant systems imply by their name that some thought went into the selection or design of the expenditure before it was released to a grantee. Evidence that a grant is strategic in nature can be found in its origination. If a grant or initiative begins its life in a written annual strategic plan or is clearly a derivative of an overarching written philosophy, it should be considered strategic. This distinguishing feature clearly separates strategic grantmaking from purely responsive grantmaking or emergency spending. This process produces relatively larger grants over longer periods of time. It demands more accountability and clear metrics to measure progress. Finally, it requires a consistently higher degree of attention and engagement from the donor (13).

Transom Systems

Transom or responsive grant mechanisms are not typically as carefully matched to the overall strategy of the donor. This form of processing relies on the periodic application for funding by a wider range of nonprofits typically using forms and approaches spelled out in advance by the donor. The strength of responsive grantmaking is clear by its name. It processes applications that are reactive to the needs of the community and it fosters innovative community-based suggestions that reflect the particular moment.

Responsive grantmaking produces more mid-sized or small grants over shorter periods of time. Depending on the style of the donor or of the associated grant product, responsive grantmaking is likely to have a moderate interest in measurement. The foundation staff gives less attention to the grantee if for no other reason than the staff did not design the proposed intervention. Responsive systems are used by a wide range of funders with a particularly close affinity among smaller organizations with few staff or with an underlying distrust of experts.

Requests For Proposals

Requests-for-proposal (RFP) processes represent a hybrid bureaucratic function somewhere between a purely strategic process and a purely responsive process. The basics of a proposed intervention are developed by the donor or foundation staff (often using carefully researched literature or experts) but the final selection of the grantee is more closely akin to responsive systems in that the grantee must react to the RFP to qualify.

Some RFPs are very complex, describing the intervention in great detail. Others are more generalized to allow for a wider range of responses. The pool of potential respondents can be pre-certified on the basis of prior similar experience, size, or internal capacity. RFPs are generally used by larger foundations with staff and a willingness to engage specialized expertise.

Discretionary Systems

Discretionary grant procedures are more closely aligned with the short-term opportunities presented by nonprofits in the environment and are usually much smaller and more charitable in form than either strategic grants, transom grants, or RFPs. Expenditures under discretionary procedures are usually short term or one-time grants that grantees find easy to request. These procedures are relatively ill-defined and are often issued without the support of formalized systems. Discretionary systems are common in family foundations and rare in highly structured organizations or public bureaucracies.

Directed or advised procedures tend to reflect the highly individualistic nature of the donor or separate family members or members of the board of directors. Grants that originate in a directed procedure can typically be issued on the authority of one person or a small group. A parallel process is the single, most common system among community foundations known as "donor-advised". These grants are usually small, short-term, easy to access, and as wide-ranging as the varied interests of the parties.

The nonprofit community generally likes directed grants because these processes are less structured. There is rarely an associated measurement or even a progress report from the grantee. Directed procedures are more common in community foundations and in smaller, family or closely held corporate foundations.

Uniform Processes

Uniform processes are the most mechanistic of all grant systems. This procedure simply divides a grant fund into many equal parts and money is issued to qualifying nonprofits without the need for an application, measurement, monitoring, or response. Uniform grant disbursement systems require little more internal bureaucracy than a checkbook. These processes are found rarely but almost always in small, highly pre-scribed family foundations wherein the original donor was extremely pre-cise in the type and nature of permissible spending.

Implications of Grant Processes

Rarely are all grant handling systems found in one organization. The choice of one system over another often varies by the size and type of foundation. Strategic systems are more likely to be found in large, inde-pendent foundations while discretionary or directed systems are found in community foundations or in smaller, family-oriented foundations. A case can be made, however, that the characteristics of each or all ap-proaches can be useful depending on the context of the mission and the funder's desired outcomes. Regardless, it is likely that the bureaucracy of the foundation grows with each added process. Finding the appropri-ate balance between intentions and structure is not impossible as more processes are adopted within the same organization (43).

As observed in other industries, foundations that grow either in size or age, may experience a maturation in their emphasis on grant processes from supporting small, short-term, and simple grants toward large, long-term, complex grants (44; 45; 46). As they age, some foundations even abandon grantmaking entirely in favor of directly operating their own ser-vice delivery program. Whether this shift in process occurs because they want to achieve the desired outcomes or out of frustration over the slow responses that come from social interventions is debatable.

Grant Products: Different Types & Styles

Business creates, modifies, or abandons products in response to their commercial value (47). Foundations, however, create grant products untethered to the natural meter of a profit (3). In such an environment, grant types are largely the product of mimicking behaviors, demand from grantees, donor proclivity, or funder capacities (13; 48). The type of grants or grant products offered has changed over time from general operating grants to more project-oriented grants.

Experience and observation indicate that at least five grant product types are commonly used by grantmaking foundations including programmatic, operating, core, capital, endowment (18). These grant types can also be segmented by the term of the grant from a single one-time grantee payment to a multi-year commitment. Some grant types are found more frequently in foundations with strategic processes and others are found in foundations with responsive or discretionary systems.

Programmatic Grants

Programmatic grants are interventions characterized by their attention to results. These grants are typically clearly defined, measurable, time-limited, closely monitored, and outcome-oriented. The criticism of programmatic grantmaking is that it provides an unstable flow of funds, programmatic uncertainty, wasted efforts, and a lack of long-term views on the part of nonprofits and funders alike (13). These grants are the most business-like in their approach to social intervention and require a high level of donor engagement.

Operating Grants

Operating grants are less tied to a beginning and ending project and more attuned to the underlying mission and function of the nonprofit grantee. These grants are used to deepen the staff and improve capacity in addition to helping insure the sustainability of the organization. Fewer restrictions are place on the uses of funds through operating grants. These grants require a lower level of engagement by the donor and are a favorite of mid-sized and small foundations.

96

Core Funding Grants

Core funding grants are an old-style approach based on trust between the grantee and the funder with the funds spent largely at the discretion of the recipient. Core grants are usually longer term and add stability to the grantee. These grants are generally easy to manage with few metrics outside of macro indictors at the business unit level. Core grants are often invitational by nature and not the sort of grant that nonprofits can simply apply to receive. They are usually given after a good track record has been established between the funder and grantee.

Capital Grants

Capital grants are provided for the purchase of buildings, equipment, technology, and land. Almost any capital good has a long term life. Capital grants are large by nature and, outside of process evaluations such as construction schedules; they are not attached to on-going metrics. The level of engagement by the donor is variable with some being quite involved for the duration of the capital project and others being very hands-off as part of a larger capital campaign such as one might see in a college or university.

Endowment Grants

Endowment grants are almost always larger and long-term with lump payments or drawn-out commitments for annual funding up to a pledged maximum. Endowments are blocks of funds that are under the control and ownership of the grantee; these are highly sought and relatively rare. Endowment grants are usually the tool of large foundations or of capital-like campaigns that consolidate many smaller grants from numerous donors.

Earnings from invested endowments provide a stable source of revenue for nonprofits and provide durability to the grantee in stressful financial times or when the work of the grantee requires the bravery that comes from stable sources of income. Many foundations prefer to keep and invest their money rather than grant large blocks to support a specific nonprofit in the belief that they can manage the money better and to keep the nonprofit's performance at the highest level. Endowments require very little engagement from the donor and are difficult to attach to short-term performance metrics.

Implications of Grant Products

The effects of each of these grant products are somewhat modified if the grant is for a single year or for multiple years, if matching donations are required, or any of several other incentive schemes such as "last dollar". Single year grants are most useful to donors for capital, endowment, or programmatic efforts such as research or planning grants. Multi-year payments (or pledges) are more useful for large-impact longitudinal projects. Core funding and operating grants are also perfectly suited for multi-year commitments where the level of engagement required of the funder is higher. However, funders are skittish about making too many multi-year commitments because they tend to limit liquidity if investable assets fall.

The choice of grant product can imply a better or worse grant process and may function more or less effectively under one giving style (see below) or another. Ideally, the grant process, type, timing, and donor style are all carefully aligned to match the funder's mission and desired outcome(s)

Styles of Giving & Levels of Engagement

Seven or more giving styles have been identified in the literature but these distinctions have not been widely adopted as helpful distinctions for analysis because donor motivations are not nearly as cleanly divided into groups. Some contend that donor styles are fixed from a lifetime of non-philanthropic experiences and are not easily adjusted to fit changing circumstances while others propose that giving styles are adjusted depending on the cause (13).

The numerous attempts to explain and predict giving by styles attests to the widely held perception that the style of the donor is an important ingredient in philanthropy. If the style of the donor is responsive to external conditions, why not several different styles in one foundation with multiple grant products and processes? This question will be explored later but first, a description of styles.

The Dynast

The Dynast represents a donor who inherited wealth from a prior generation and who gives along traditional family lines. Dynasts are largely
found in private family foundations or family-owned and operated businesses. Strict Dynasts probably look for grant products that do not require high levels of engagement and simpler grant processes such as
uniform, transom, directed, or discretionary. With enough financial capacity, Dynasts could be interested in capital or even endowment products and they are likely to be willing to undertake multi-year projects.

The Communitarian

The Communitarian represents a donor focused on geography, race,
gender, or geo-political groups. Communitarians should be willing to be
more engaged in their grantmaking if for no other reason than grants to
any defined population carriy inherent complexities. They are probably
willing to undertake more strategic processes and may even mix processes more freely. Their interests will span multiple processes and several grant products at the same time across several years.

The Repayer

The Repayer is a donor with an interest in repaying a kindness or a service. A good example of a Repayer is the university alumni. Repayers
are likely to be interested in few focused processes such as uniform or
directed. They may have a tendency to shy away from complex strategies and multi-year commitments and will focus on highly flexible grant
products such as operating or core funding.

The Devoutist

The Devout donor gives from a basically religious orientation. Donations
that support a Devoutist's religious preference and belief system could
be multi-year and easily attracted by similarly affiliated nonprofits. Devoutists understand leaps of faith and are likely to be more willing to fund
endowments, core grants, capital, and operating grant products. Processes attractive to Devoutists are likely to use simpler grant processes
that permit flexibility within their religious sphere such as directed or discretionary. If the mission and desired outcomes are in a religiously affili-

ated sphere, Devoutists may even consider adopting more complex processes such as might work for a group of Methodist hospitals or Catholic universities, etc.

The Investor

The Investor makes donations primarily for the self-serving tax benefit. This donor is likely to use a single process and only one or two grant products with single-year terms. Investors might gravitate toward variable low-engagement approaches such as capital, endowment, or core and a whimsical discretionary process.
The Socialite

The Socialite donates in response to the norms of a certain social class. Socialites value flexible systems such as discretionary or directed processes but may, depending on the economic class in which they circulate, be very interested in strategic, transom, and RFP approaches. Socialites could have a wide range of grant products from capital to endowments and programmatic but this is probably more closely correlated to the size of their foundation as a proxy measure for their social circles. Metrics are probably of less interest but they could have multi-year distributions with substantial invested assets on which to base a longer term program.

The Altruist

The Altruist gives in order to find meaning. This is a relatively rare approach implying a very mature viewpoint and great confidence. Altruists are likely to be interested in impact and outcome clarity and, therefore, metrics, measurement, and evaluation systems. Basic processes could include strategic and transom with large endowments and discretionary, directed, and uniform processes if the foundation asset base is smaller. Grant products could lean more towards core and programmatic grants so long as the impact of their spending is targeting a desperate need. Altruists are less likely to be interested in funding programs that are without obvious effects on relieving suffering such as planning grants, research grants, the arts, and economic development. The degree of engagement in the grant program by the Altruist could be quite high.

The Venturist

The Venture donor applies extensive business skills, is very interested in metrics and accountability, and willing to make large, long-term financial commitments if the funded project has a decent chance of being widely adopted. The Venture funder is probably very willing to be highly engaged in the grantmaking process, to help apply business skills to social settings, and to keep the programs moving on schedule. They are probably willing to undertake more strategic processes and may even mix processes more freely. Their interests will span multiple processes and several grant products at the same time across several years.

Fitting Process & Product to Grant Style

With some modification to accommodate the field of philanthropy, contingency theory suggests that a foundation that offers grant products and processes commensurate with its size and in relationship to its mission/ outcome will perform better than one that does not make this adjustment. As expected, this theory has been difficult to test in the world of metric-free philanthropy.

A worthwhile exercise for any foundation is to identify the mission and desired outcome(s) for say five years into the future, and then to design the processes and products that offer the most opportunities for success given its size. This advantage of this approach is that it offers a methodology supported by theory and recent research. After completion of the exercise, a grantee-based systematic feedback instrument could indicate if grantees observed improved foundation effectiveness.

Grant Process & Product Applied To Giving Style

GRANT PROCESS	GIVING STYLE							
	Dynast	Communitarian	Repayer	Devoutist	Investor	Socialite	Altruist	Venturist
Strategic		a,b,c,d,e					a,b,c,d,e	a,b,c,d,e
Transom	a	a,b,c,d				b,c,d,e	a,b,c,d	
RFP		a					a,b,c,d	a,b
Discretionary	abcd	a,b	c	b,c,d,e	b,c,d	c,e	a,b,c,d	
Directed	ab	b	b,d	b,c,d,e	b,c,d	c	a,b,c,d	
Uniform	d		b,d		b,d		b,d	

Grant Products Table Key:

a	b	c	d	e
Programmatic	Operating	Core	Capital	Endowment

Table 1: Grant Products Aligned With Style and Process

Key Points To Remember:

- As the size of a foundation increases, it tends to act more like a business and adopt more sophisticated processes.

- The larger the foundation, the more likely it is to be a failure.

- Evidence that a grant is strategic in nature can be found in its origination.

- The choice of one system of handling grants over another system often varies by the size and type of foundation.

- Observation indicates at least five grant product types are commonly used by grantmaking foundations including programmatic, operating, core, capital, and endowment.

- The choice of grant product can imply a better or worse grant process and may function more or less effectively under one giving style or another.

- A foundation that offers grant products and processes commensurate with its size and in relationship to its mission/desired-outcome will perform better than one that does not make this adjustment.

- A worthwhile exercise for any foundation is to identify the mission and desired outcome(s) for up to five years, and then to design the processes and products that offer the most opportunities for success given its size.

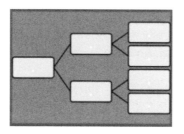

CHAPTER ELEVEN

Concept Mapping for Grantmakers

Concept Mapping: Theory vs. Practice

Concept Mapping is the graphic depiction of an assumptive cause-and-effect relationship between two or more measurable constructs based on a mix of imperfect objective and subjective information. A complete example of a full concept map has been printed on the inside of the *Supercharged Giving* dust cover. Concept Mapping often assumes a stronger cause-and-effect relationship than can be proven from the literature; rather, it explains the funder's reasoning for making specific grants.

Concept Mapping is the natural extension of the strategic thinking process explained in detail in the preceding two parts of *Supercharged Giving*. Without using the strategic approach described in earlier chapters, Concept Mapping cannot achieve its maximum impact for funders. The best way to illustrate the power of Concept Mapping is through a series of examples developed for the mythical "XYZ-Foundation". Any resemblance of the "XYZ" Foundation to a real organization is accidental and unintended.

Perfect knowledge being elusive, the ideal circumstance rarely exists in practice. Grantmakers must therefore frequently settle for an assumption of cause-and-effect based on imperfect knowledge unsupported by precise empirical evidence that fits their circumstances (15). In more practical terms, Concept Mapping is a snapshot that demonstrates the grantmaker's beliefs, assumptions, and hopes for certain outcomes resulting from a specific grant expenditure. It rests on the more technical but widely misunderstood "theory of change" described in Part Two of *Supercharged Giving* (21).

Strategy, or "theory of change" may best be described as the underlying belief of the donor or foundation of "What" the problem is that is the focus of their grantmaking. It demonstrates their reasoning about how to solve the problem (21). Having and applying a "theory of change" is one of the core principles of strategic philanthropy described in Part One; it is how the foundation believes it will positively impact society (20). As practiced by grantmakers, "theory of change" is not particularly objective; it can be argued that it emphasizes the subjectivity of philanthropists (23). Theory of change is actually a fusion of two separate approaches: (1) evidence drawn from the literature, and (2) subjective opinion, ideology, and beliefs. For this reason, Concept Mapping is more akin to a descriptive language than a scientific statement of fact.

Definition 12: Concept Mapping

Concept Mapping is the graphic depiction of an assumptive cause-and-effect relationship between two or more measurable constructs based on a mix of imperfect objective and subjective information.

A recent survey of one hundred of the largest foundations in the United States (based on annual qualifying distributions), found that only about half of the surveyed practitioners understood the term "theory of change" (21). The term is often applied at the level of single projects but at other times it is applied at the "enterprise" or foundation-wide level. Regardless of the unit of application, the field of philanthropy has largely accepted that its effectiveness and ultimate value rests in adopting some means of connecting their intentions to their grants (13).

Although a "theory of change" is sometimes confused with a "logic model", there is a clear distinction between the two concepts. As discussed in Part One, a "logic model" is the sum of inputs, processes, and outputs of a grant, while "theory of change" is the reasoning that drives

106

the "logic model" (17). For example, as a "theory of change" a funder might believe that by improving the skills of classroom teachers, they will subsequently improve the achievement level of the teacher's students. The "logic model" applied to this theory would consist of a series of inputs (new curricula, stipends, books, instruction from a master teacher, etc.), a process (weekend classes for teachers), and an outcome (better educated students) all of which might result in improved student achievement.

Graphic Communications: a Universal Language

A picture is worth a thousand words (49). A picture can communicate a complex story or a set of relationships in a quickly understandable way. The popularity of graphics to pictorially display relationships can be seen in various fields including engineering, physics, and chemistry among others. Graphic design is used to create a picture of a series of known or suspected relationships. The picture can be used to show a static relationship frozen in time, or it can show a very dynamic set of relationships that change with various different assumptions and theories. So, graphic communications can produce a picture of relationships as they existed in the past, as they appear in the present, or as they can be hypothesized and projected into the future.

Today, this field is known as "info-graphics" which is a simplifying visual language for very complex information (50). Computer icons are good examples of modern info-graphics. The icons are part of a form of visual literacy which has developed into a universal pictorial language used in computers around the world regardless of the spoken language.

Graphic Theory

Graphic language continues to evolve and spread to new disciplines. As an example, before the 1980's, newspapers made very little use of graphics to tell stories whereas modern newspapers such as *The Wall Street Journal*, and *USA Today* now use graphic language extensively. Pictures for words---info-graphical techniques---have created an international, universal language that can be found in newspapers, magazines, outdoor billboards, and even labels on the door to the restroom. Advances are being pioneered by graphic linguists such as Nigel Holmes who recently proposed a new way of binary pairing that may eventually be used to graphically depict the "best" of everything, even among the most subjective of issues (51). In the spirit of these trends, the world is in for a growing graphic language that will be capable of depicting and simplifying almost any item or relationship and philanthropy will be no exception to the trend. Concept Mapping is just the beginning of a new shorthand language for philanthropists that can easily show the theoretical connections between the mission of the organization or donor and the expected outcome of a grant or gift.

Causality: The Weak Link

In chaos theory, there is a term known as the "butterfly effect." It is short -hand for a complex notion of "sensitive dependence on initial conditions" wherein small variations at the beginning of a dynamical system (such as the weather), can produce outsized changes in the behavior of that system (52). According to the theory, when a butterfly flaps its wings in Tahiti, a tornado forms in Kansas (53). This hypothesized relationship lacks any directly observed evidence of causality but it is a good example of a very simplified picture of a complex system. For private foundations, pinning down "causality" as a basis for any particular theory of change in the social sciences is as elusive as proving the "butterfly effect".

Causality describes the relationship between one event (the cause) and another event (the effect) which is the direct consequence or result of the cause (54). Causality is difficult, even impossible, to prove in the social sciences because there are simply too many confounding primary and secondary contributing causes to most problems. Regardless, Concept Mapping is based on a field of causation study known as "Root Cause Analysis" (RCA). RCA attempts to identify the root causes of observable problems or events. Grantmakers trying to solve problems by eliminating root causes (as opposed to just the symptoms) would be taking an RCA approach. RCA is not a sharply defined process. It is considered to be the product of a management approach known as "continuous improvement" that is used in many complex manufacturing processes aimed at reducing product defects or improving product quality.

The point is that grantmakers and donors operate on the basis of assumptions about causality that are difficult to prove. The value of Concept Mapping is as a communication tool that displays the assumed relationship between two or more variables. It shows a particular combination of (1) reasoning by a grantmaker, (2) "best methods" found in the literature, and (3) opinions of various community leaders.

Concept Mapping Demonstrated

Supercharged Giving proposes that every grant paid by a foundation should have a clear, understandable relationship to the foundation's mission. Whether that donor is a corporation, private, or family foundation, health legacy foundation, or individual, the intent of the gift should be clearly stated and the desired outcome should be measurable. Mission statements, principals, goals, or objectives by these or other names answer one fundamentally important question. These statements define "What" the grantmaker is trying to accomplish and they describe the reason that the organization exists. These statements provide direction, limitation, authority, and justification for the actions the foundation takes or doesn't take.

Concept Maps© begin with the mission of the organization as "level 1". Depending on the complexity of the organization, the mission, strategies, goals, and objectives can involve as many as eight levels.

Level 1: Mission
Level 2: Strategies
Level 3: Goals
Level 4: Goal Components
Level 5: Objectives
Level 6: Objective Components
Level 7: Action Plans
Level 8: Budgets

These eight levels are shown in the graphic on the next page.

The best way to demonstrate how a Concept Map works is through an illustrative example. Assume that the mythical private foundation known as the "XYZ-Foundation" wants to improve the life of children in its community. This project, named the "Nurse Practitioner Project" is mapped on the next few pages.

Graphic 33: Theoretical Design of A Concept Map

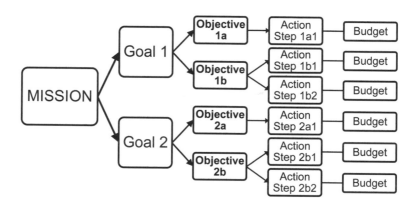

Sample Concept Map: The Nurse Practitioner Project

Level 1: Mission

The "XYZ Foundation" is interested in a very broad mission to create a "quality community for children". Its mission statement could start with a basic structure that helps define "community". This might be a geographic location or a community of people such as "all children" or both. This element should be limiting to the extent it is helpful in containing the work of the foundation and explaining that work in simple terms to interested parties. More expansive examples of community could be "all users of the world wide web" or "all women and girls living in the United States", so the mission can go from tiny to gargantuan at this early stage. The term "quality", being difficult to define, also needs some clarity. A first draft of the mission follows.

Text Box 1: Example Rough Draft Mission Statement

XYZ-Foundation will improve the quality of life for children in New Orleans, Louisiana.

Many organizations like the poetry of this type of mission statement. For a start, the term "quality" is now limited to a certain group. The target population is "children", and the geographic location of the work is now focused on the city of "New Orleans". However, an effective mission statement should at least infer a way to measure progress. Such clarity need not detract from the beauty and the poetic flow of the statement. Perhaps "quality" could be structured in such a way as to also be measurable?

Quality of Life Defended

Following more research, the "XYZ Foundation" discovered that many of the most important parameters of child health can be measured using a multi-dimensional instrument focused on the quality of life. This time, the draft mission statement is a little more precise.

Text   Box   2:   Improved   Rough   Draft   Mission   Statement

> **XYZ-Foundation** will improve the physical, material, emotional, and social well-being of children living in New Orleans, Louisiana.

Evidence also suggests that quality of life indicators can be developed for isolated populations such as "children", and the staff discovers several cities already use a quality of life model as a proxy to measure health status.

With a little more digging, the staff of XYZ-Foundation documented the pitifully poor quality of life among the children living with parents who earn incomes in the bottom quartile of all families in New Orleans. It was subsequently suggested that the mission be modified to capture this connection.

Text Box 3: XYZ-Foundation Mission Statement

> **XYZ-Foundation** will improve the physical, material, emotional, and social well-being of children in families living in poverty in New Orleans, Louisiana.

Following these revisions, the new mission statement is a clearer, more precise description of that the foundation wants to do.

Mission to Outcomes: Defining Success

For purposes of the example, the shorthand term for the mission statement is: "Well-Being of Children". The board of directors of the XYZ-Foundation imagined the desired outcome of its grantmaking as if it already achieved its mission.

The members decided that the desired outcome would improve children's lives in four areas in ten years: (1) access to affordable health care, (2) family stability and income, (3) safety, and (4) social strengthening. This is an important step because the linkage between the mission and the desired outcome helps create a vision for the organization looking ten years into the future.

With a vision defined, the foundation could clearly state a measurable statement of what success would look like in a few years.

Graphic 34: Foundation Outcomes Imagined

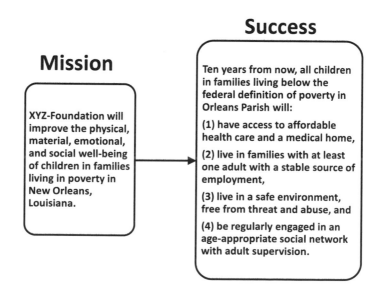

Level 2: Mission To Strategy

Concept Mapping graphically depicts the known or suspected relationships between goals, strategies, objectives, and tactics down to and
including individual grants. It provides a shorthand language that explains why a donation was made, and the expected measurable result.
Recall from Part One that a strategy is similar to a "theory of change".
It documents the reasoning that connects the mission statement to the
goal statements and thence to objectives, action steps and budgets to
the desired outcome(s).

Strategies ultimately lead to outcomes but not always the desired outcomes. An important weakness in adopting any strategy is that a
causal relationship is assumed between the actions and the results.
The relationship can be positive (more of one action increase the outcome) or negative (more of one action decreases the outcome). Most
assumptions about causality are weak even with the latest research
but such assumptions are still better than uninformed guesstimates.

The XYZ-Foundation has chosen to pursue three strategies described
on the next page. They will issue grants, operate the foundation effi-
ciently, and invest foundation funds prudently. These three strategies
are almost universal among grantmaking foundations. Other strategies
could be to "deliver a specified service" as an operating foundation
might do or to "increase the endowment" as a community foundation
would hope to accomplish.

XYZ-Foundation Strategies

In other words, the foundation believes that grants paid to nonprofit
organizations will be an effective way to achieve its mission. The
grantmaking strategy adopted by the board includes four important
functions of the work first identified by Porter and specifically states:

"XYZ-Foundation will use a grantmaking strategy to:

(1) Strategically identify and fund nonprofit organizations operating
promising programs producing results that address one or more barriers to achieving its desired outcome;

(2) Evaluate the performance of funded programs and hold grantees accountable for results; and

(3) Direct the attention of other funders and the community to successful programs in order to influence the efficient use of other scarce charitable resources."

Graphic 35: Concept Map Mission to Strategy

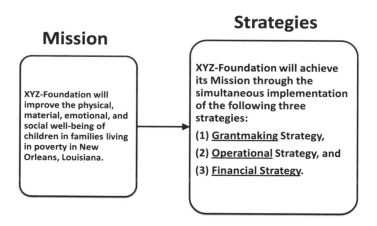

Graphic 36: XYZ-Foundation Grantmaking Strategy

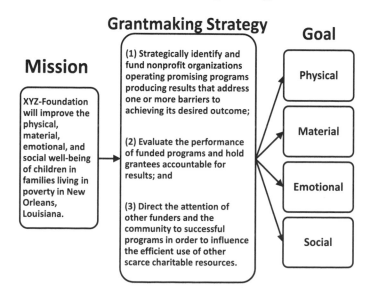

The next graphic depicts the Operational Strategy and details three functions including (1) efficiency, (2) relationships, and (3) measurement. The second depicts the Financial Strategy with three detailed components including: (1) investing, (2) auditing, and (3) budgeting.

Graphic 37: Operational Strategy Defined

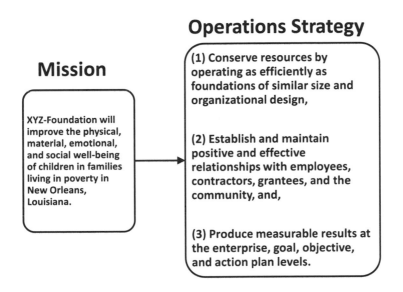

Like "grantmaking", these two strategies are also directly linked to the mission of the XYZ-Foundation and could be unconventionally considered to be supporting theories of change. Without effective financial and operational strategies, the grantmaking strategy eventually runs out of money or staff support or both.

Graphic 38: Financial Strategy Defined

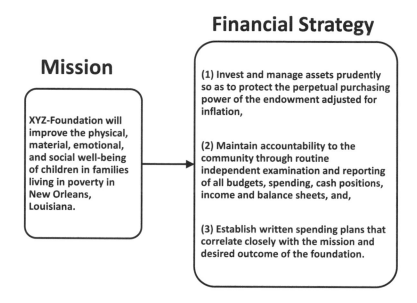

Level 3: Mission To Goals

In theory, when all goals are accomplished, the mission is completed and should be abandoned or modified to reflect those achievements. An example of a nonprofit organization achieving and then subsequently modifying its mission is the March of Dimes. Organized originally to fight childhood polio, once that dreaded disease was defeated, it changed its mission to the broader category of "birth defects". Therefore, the goal statements should be a balance between broad, general terms that are difficult to measure (poetry) and more measurable specific terms (prose). After a group-ranking exercise, the board also assigned priorities to each goal area or "zone of interest" with "Physical" well-being ranked as the most important.

The XYZ-Foundation mission statement divides neatly into four grant-making subsections: Physical Well-Being, Material Well-Being, Emotional Well-being, and Social Well-Being. Each subsection provides a neat folder or divider for the identification of four separate a grantmaking goals associated with the mission of the "Well-Being of Children".

Graphic 39: Concept Map Mission to Goals

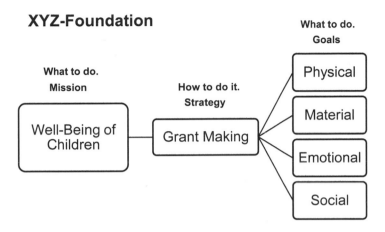

XYZ-Foundation examined the literature in each of these four goal areas or "zones of interest" and adopted a series of goals taking into consideration the community context. The function of a goal is to act as a major sub-set of the mission to help clarify and contain a working definition for each zone of interest such as "Physical Health" which would otherwise be too ill-defined to measure or to know if the Foundation made any headway in achieving its mission.

Following the advice found in Chapter Two, the XYZ-Foundation completed a community needs assessment as part of its research and in preparation for answering the "Why" question. Why does the XYZ-Foundation target children in families living in poverty in New Orleans? The major indicators of the well-being of children indicated they were in dire straits with a large portion living in poverty, an unusually high infant mortality rate, a higher than average incidence of childhood illnesses, and single-family parents.

Level 4: Goal Components

In order to clearly articulate its goals, the XYZ-Foundation adopted four separate goal statements (one for each zone of interest found in its mission statement). In developing the goal statement for children's "Physical" well-being, the possible range of activities was so extensive that almost any specific grant even remotely related could fit the title. The XYZ-Foundation clearly needed to reduce the universe of possible grant programs even further to be effective and to avoid spreading its money and talent across an overly broad range.

Table 2: Example of Too Much To Do

Sub-Categories Childhood Physical Well-Being
• Abuse
• Healthcare Access
• Prevention of Disease & Injury
• Early Screening & Intervention
• Basic Healthcare Education
• Family Stability
• Food & Nutrition
• Learning Readiness
• Nurturing Relationships
• Parental Preparedness
• Physical Activity
• Social Interaction
• Toxicity & Hazards

Grouping a seemingly inexhaustible list of possible health-related topics focused on children's physical well-being into a reduced set of commonly held factors produced a much smaller list of possible grantmaking activities. However, this list was still too broad and difficult to measure. To narrow the goal, board members suggested that the target population could be reduced to children under the age of six. But, a majority of the board wanted to select the most important sub-categories as a framework to reduce the scope of the goal; still others wanted to give up on the idea of measurement entirely.

After consulting the recently completed needs assessment and conducting a focus group of local low-income parents, the XYZ-Foundation decided to prioritize the possible categories based on those items that impact parents and the very youngest children the most. This approach re-organized and reduced the list from 13 items to five major factors.

Table 3: Seeking Clarity in Childhood Well-Being

Sub-Categories Childhood Physical Well-Being
• Healthcare Access
• Prevention of Disease & Injury
• Early Screening & Intervention
• Food & Nutrition
• Toxicity & Hazards

Finally, a small committee was appointed to draft a goal for the childhood "Physical" well-being zone of interest which produced the following statement.

Text Box 4: Physical Well-Being Goal Statement

Goal Statement: Childhood Physical Well-Being
Children living in poverty in New Orleans, Louisiana, will enjoy increased physical well-being through improved access to healthcare, disease and injury prevention, early screening and intervention, healthy food and nutrition, and freedom from toxic and hazardous living conditions.

The Concept Map for XYZ-Foundation could be refined to a new, more specific level based on the goal statement. Although there are many additional grantmaking opportunities, the foundation has chosen to limit its work (and thus to further define its mission) by channeling its efforts into five factors including healthcare access, injury prevention, early screening, food & nutrition, and toxicity & hazards. These five "Major Goal Factors" were extracted from the goal statement and formed the structure for the next lower (fourth) level of the example Concept Map.

Noting the difficulties with causality mentioned earlier in this chapter, the sample Concept Map with four levels graphically depicts the relationship that XYZ-Foundation assumes exists between the mission, grantmaking strategy, zones of interest, and goal statements as shown next. To save space, the mission statement, also known as "Level 1", has been removed but all maps eventually connect to the mission.

Graphic 40: Mapping Mission to Goal Components

After adopting a goal statement for "Childhood Physical Well-Being", the XYZ-Foundation researched the major issues involved in each major factor and defined, debated, and prioritized the factors. As the example continues, the major goal factor of "Healthcare Access" yielded several possible functional clusters including human capital, health facilities, health insurance, public policies, and health literacy. While there were many other possible components of "Healthcare Access", the literature supported these five as the components with the greatest impact on children.

Level 5: Mission To Objectives

The fifth level Concept Map for "Physical Well-Being of Children" was added to the XYZ-Foundation business plan. The first term "Human Capital" can be expanded into a detailed written objective and can be adjusted each year based on a combination of the literature, past achievements of the foundation, and changing foundation preferences.

XYZ-Foundation Sample Objectives

The board and management of XYZ-Foundation decided to concentrate a portfolio of grants in the "Human Capital" component. Interviews with the local school of medicine, the nursing school and the school of allied health indicated a desperate need for pediatricians and pediatric nurse practitioners in the federally under-served region.

Graphic 41: Mapping Mission to Objectives

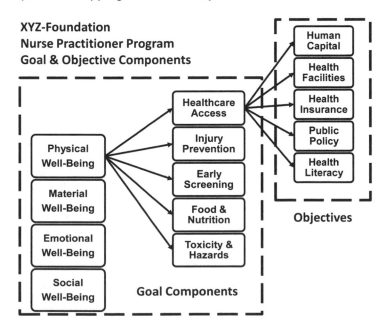

Text Box 5: Example Nurse Practitioner Project Objective

Objective: New Nurse Practitioner Program

By the end of the fiscal year, management will propose a short-term plan to increase the number of pediatric nurse practitioners working in the region from seven to twenty and a long-term plan resulting in a new graduate degree-granting nursing program in collaboration with ABC College School of Nursing (Responsible Party: Jane Doe, Program Officer).

Level Six: Objective Components

The new objective is written to describe two temporal components. Clearly, it encompasses a short-term recruitment element and a long-term training element. The new Concept Map now shows this temporal division.

Graphic 42: Mapping Objective Components

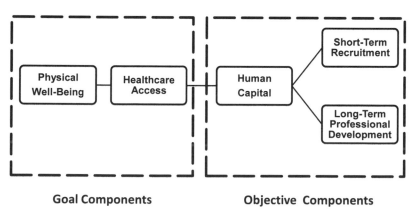

The Foundation also discovered that there was no pediatric nurse practitioner training program in the region. They realized the program would not be successful without the support of the county pediatric and medical societies. After several months of negotiation, the parties agreed to support an initial class for pediatric nurse practitioners at the local four-year college. Unfortunately, the college did not offer a master's degree in nursing which is the type of advanced degree nurses need to move into the nurse practitioner role.

Level Seven: Action Steps

After a protracted series of discussions, the local college and the state board of higher education agreed to a new advanced nursing practice program focused on pediatrics. The first class 12 students was authorized a year later. With facilities for training in short supply, the foundation partnered with another private foundation that specialized in capital projects to renovate an existing building on the college campus near the medical center. An example of action steps for the "Human Capital" element of the "Nurse Practitioner" objectives includes five short-term action plans and three long-term action plans.

Text Box 6: Nurse Practitioner Action Step "Timetable"

> **Timetable:** By January 31, develop a written timetable for the recruitment of faculty and practitioners such that recruitment takes advantage of college breaks and semester assignments.

Text Box 7: Nurse Practitioner Action Step "Pay & Incentives"

> **Pay & Incentives:** By February 15, engage a compensation specialist to advise on the development of externally competitive and internally equitable pay and incentives in collaboration with the area hospital and local clinics.

Text Box 8: Nurse Practitioner Action Step "Recruiting Firm"

> **Recruiting Firm:** By March 1, advertise for and complete the selection of a professional recruitment firm with specialized skills in the medical field to initiate a search for a nursing faculty chair and one additional key faculty plus thirteen or more additional nurse practitioners in the area.

Graphic 43: Nurse Practitioner Mission to Action Plans

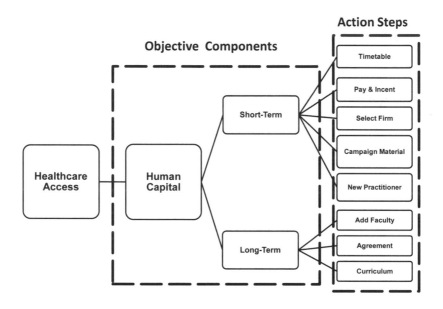

Text Box 9: Nurse Practitioner Action Step "Campaign"

Campaign Materials: By March 15, design, write, print and stock nurse recruitment campaign materials and identify target mailing population of faculty and practitioners for initiation of campaign April 15 for fall semester.

Text Box 10: Nurse Practitioner Action Step "Recruit"

Recruit Initial Faculty & Practitioners: By June 1, recruit key faculty chair and additional nursing provost by August 1 with parallel practitioner recruitment project resulting in 6 new practitioners in the region by September and an additional 7 by the end of the year.

Text Box 11:Nurse Practitioner Action Step "Additional Faculty"

Recruit Additional Faculty: By first quarter of year two, recruit additional three faculty members and begin curriculum design.

Text Box 12: Nurse Practitioner Action Step "Agreement"Text Box 13:

Agreement: By March 1, complete master agreement with ABC College to establish a graduate nurse practitioner training program including identification of temporary faculty and teaching space and long term facilities for renovation.

Nurse Practitioner Action Step "Initial Curriculum"

Initial Curriculum: By May 15 of second year, complete curriculum development and submit a draft to the state board of nursing supported by ABC College and new faculty chair.

Level 8: Budgets

An example of a series of action plan budgets developed by the staff of XYZ-Foundation demonstrated that the initiative had blossomed into a much more complex and strategically connected series of activities than the board at first envisioned.

Table 4: Example Nurse Practitioner Action Plan Budget

Tactical Budget Objective: Nurse Practitioner Project									
Short-Term Recruitment Budget									
Timetable		Pay & Incentives		Recruiting Firm		Campaign		Recruit		Grand Total
Item	Cost	Item	Cost	Item	Cost	Item	Cost	Item	Cost	
Travel	$300	Travel	$1,200	Travel	$3,000	Travel	$15,000	Travel	$20,000	$39,500
Lodging	$300	Lodging	$700	Lodging	$4,000	Lodging	$10,000	Lodging	$12,000	$27,000
Meals	$100	Meals	$500	Meals	$1,500	Meals	$2,500	Meals	$4,000	$8,600
Meetings	$600	Meetings	$500	Meetings	$500	Meetings	$1,500	Meetings	$2,000	$5,100
Transcript	$100	Consultant	$4,000			Media 1	$500	Bonuses	$100,000	$104,600
Copying	$100	Report	$450			Media 2	$500	Relocation	$300,000	$301,050
Notary	$100					Media 3	$500	Media 1	$5,000	$5,600
Misc.	$100			Misc.	$1,000	Misc.	$2,000	Misc.	$5,000	$8,100
SubTotal	$1,700	SubTotal	$7,350	SubTotal	$10,000	SubTotal	$32,500	SubTotal	$448,000	$499,550

The plan had also evolved into a multi-year portfolio of grant programs starting with a new coalition with the medical society to leveraging additional funding from another sympathetic foundation. It also necessitated a capital grant to match the money promised by the new partnering foundation, and the graduate students were all working in local hospitals or clinics and needed scholarships to begin.

The Concept Map for the entire project included elements in Policy Advocacy and in Health Facilities as seen in the next map which captures the entire scope of the project with the exception of multi-year arrangements typically included in the various grant agreements.

Concept Mapping Portfolios

The following example also demonstrates a group of related strategies, objectives, and tactical action plans known as a grant "portfolio". The collective activities all relate to the Nurse Practitioner Project but use varied approaches that work in concert to achieve the desired result.

The full portfolio map contains a combination of grantmaking activities and operational activities directed by staff of the XYZ-Foundation. It includes three major objectives: "Human Capital", "Health Facilities", and "Public Policy". Each objective includes a descriptive component that is embedded in the language of the objective such as "Short-Term" or "State Higher Education Approval". Lastly, the objectives are connected to various action plans to be followed by specific budgets.

Graphic 44: Nurse Practitioner Project Map

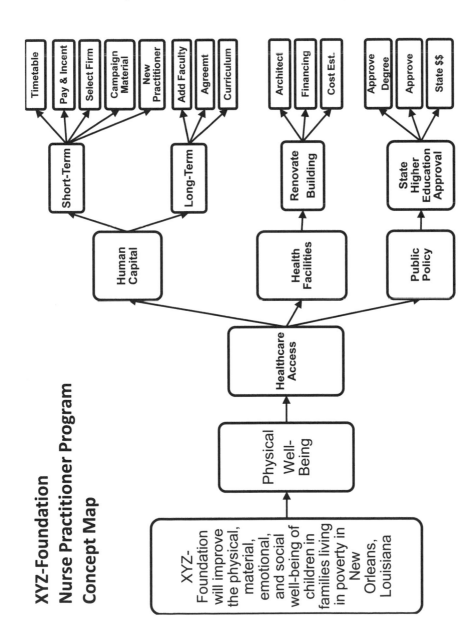

Example 2: The Child Injury Prevention Project

As a second example of Concept Mapping, an "Injury Prevention" objective was developed by XYZ-Foundation as a subset of "Physical Well-Being" for the 2009 fiscal year and the responsible party was Program Officer, "Jane Doe".

Graphic 45: XYZ-Foundation Physical Injury Prevention

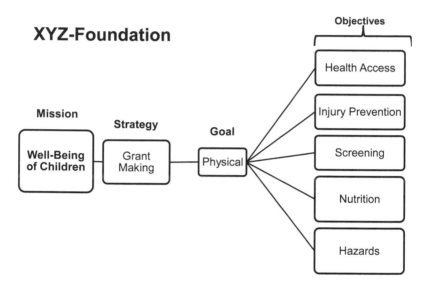

Text Box 14: Example Injury Prevention Objective

Injury Prevention. By December 31, 2009, the incidence of familial abuse of a child in Orleans Parish will be reduced from 12/1000 to the Louisiana average of 10.9/1000 by targeting the 40.5% of children living in poverty and using an interventional model developed nationally by Safe Horizons. Responsible Program Officer: Jane Doe (extension 2345).

Similar objectives were also developed for the other four categories including "Health Access", "Screening", "Nutrition", and "Hazards".

Each objective under the example "Physical Well-Being" is also supported by a series of action steps and budgets.

Graphic 46: XYZ-Foundation Injury Prevention Action Steps

XYZ-Foundation

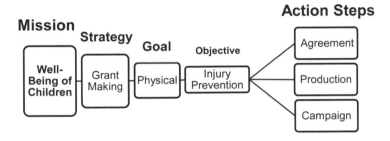

To accomplish the "Injury Prevention" objective, Jane Doe, Program Officer, has determined that an agreement should be completed between the participating parties. Afterward, she estimated that a series of three media ads should be created and produced followed by an all-media campaign targeting parents and potential abuse informants.

Text Box 15: Injury Prevention Action Step 1 "Agreement"

Agreement: Before Mardi Gras, a Memorandum of Understanding will be completed between the participants defining the roles of Safe Horizons, the Child Advocacy Center, and The Hope Shining Alliance Network.

Text Box 16: Injury Prevention Action Step 2
"Media Ad Development"

Production: By May 15, 2009, complete production of three video ads and collateral print material based on the selected interventional model.

Text Box 17: Injury Prevention Action Step 3
"Media Campaign"

Campaign: On or before September 15, 2009, launch 90-day multimedia campaign targeting parents and potential informants in 12 census codes with the highest incidence of child abuse; conclude campaign by the time general holiday advertising ends on December 23, 2009.

For each action step a budget was created by the program officer in consultation with the accounting department. The budget captured the costs of each action step in adequate detail to provide meaningful estimation. Costs were then rolled up to each successive level through the goal and mission statements for a strategic plan total.

The three budgets for the action steps also include several other cost sections including "travel", "copying", etc. shown on the next page.

Table 5: Example Injury Prevention Action Step Budget

Tactical Budget Objective: Safety						
Agreement		Production		Campaign		Grand Total
Item	Cost	Item	Cost	Item	Cost	
Travel	$600	Travel	$4,000	Travel	$400	$5,000
Lodging	$300	Lodging	$2,000	Lodging	$100	$2,400
Meals	$100	Meals	$1,100	Meals	$50	$1,250
Meetings	$600	Meetings	$400	Meetings	$250	$1,250
Transcript	$100	Equip.	$5,000	Media 1	$101,000	$106,100
Copying	$100	Lighting	$4,500	Media 2	$210,100	$214,700
Notary	$100	Editing	$3,000	Media 3	$138,000	$141,100
Misc.	$100	Talent	$12,000	Misc.	$100	$12,200
SubTotal	$2,000	SubTotal	$32,000	SubTotal	$450,000	$484,000

When to Stop Mapping

The purpose of Concept Mapping is to communicate two viewpoints:
(1) the approved viewpoint of "What to Do", and (2) the wider viewpoint
of "What Not To Do" covering the strategic approaches that were considered but rejected. The approved "What To Do" viewpoint depicts
the reasoning that connects a string of measures in the annual strategic plan beginning with the mission and ending with action steps and
budgets. The rejected "What Not To Do" viewpoint depicts the major
related concepts that have been considered but excluded from the
strategy.

These two viewpoints give the reader a clear understanding at a
glance of the expectations of the plan and the nodes at which an indicator or measure may be selected and of a few of the possible approaches that were considered but rejected. The "What Not To Do"
string of possible approaches helps put the chosen path in context with
the literature and thinking of the board and staff.

Either viewpoint can be as complex and detailed as time and space
permit. In some ways, the strategic plan is really a never ending story
simply because there is no end to the possible issues, approaches,
and theories that can be considered. So, where does Concept Mapping stop? It stops when the user is satisfied that the strategy or
"theory of change" has been adequately portrayed. The decision of
when to stop mapping is a subjective one based on the judgment of

the organization. There is no hard and fast rule.

Avoiding Bulky Bureaucracy

Many funders fear that bureaucracy will suffocate their grantmaking passions (55). Finding a proper balance between the two, however, is the real challenge. The most important ingredient for effective philanthropy rests in keeping the ultimate social goal of the foundation in mind as it goes about systematically implementing various bureaucratic processes such as Concept Mapping. Lose sight of the mission and the bureaucracy will take over. As soon as success is measured by the number and complexity of the various concept maps, or of applications reviewed and scored, or by the efficiency with which each check is printed and mailed, the "process" has won and the mission has lost. A professional philanthropist learns that it is very easy, and even beguiling, to meet the demands of complex mapping procedures before settling on the ultimate reason for making a grant. It is a temptation to be avoided or resisted.

Likewise, philanthropy is not unlike most other industries in that it falls prey to faddish tides that, from time to time, sweep out the old and usher in something new. Adopting a few of these new, unproven initiatives or approaches is tantamount to added bureaucracy because few of the old procedures are actually eliminated. Instead, the foundation simply bolts a new approach on top of an old one and maintains both mechanisms. This is an alluring way to grow bureaucracy and douse passions since it appears to be keeping the organization "au currant". Beware of these creeping fads as they are a threat to the mission of the organization over the long term.

One technique to avoid creeping bureaucracy is a rigorous self-assessment that includes feedback from grantees through independent third parties who can act as filters to protect the identity of interviewees. Another is to systematically examine the outcomes and impacts of the organization and not just of the grantees. Taken collectively, this information can be used to evaluate how effective the foundation is in keeping true to its mission. This is known as an "enterprise level" evaluation---a difficult, time-consuming and often painful self-appraisal. It's strong advantage is that it serves as an effective bureaucracy-killer which helps energize the original passion of the founders.

Obviously some bureaucracy is important if the foundation is to function effectively. A recent analysis confirmed that as much as 60% of the impact of a foundation initiative originates from the skill set of the staff versus the money in a grant (56). The management and staff of a foundation are technical experts that should add value to the design and implementation of grants or initiatives, but often do not improve the original decision of "what" to fund and why (4). Avoiding overly restrictive and inflexible rules is therefore of fundamental importance in balancing the role of the staff and the impact of the organization in the community.

It is often argued that bureaucracies have been replaced by more rapid-response entrepreneurial approaches to the delivery of services or the design of organizations (42). However, there are many examples in modern management literature of bureaucratic public and nonprofit organizations that successfully select, repress, discard, or renew systems to improve effectiveness (57). Such renewal also creates a "re-enchantment" response that keeps the organization vibrant.

Accountability is Good for All

Foundations have natural effectiveness and efficiency disadvantages compared to most business enterprises. Without stockholders, customers, or even profits, and unable to distribute earnings to a third party, foundations are only rarely held to account by outsiders (28). This accountability disadvantage can result in undisciplined channels of authority, fuzzy financial reporting, and even a complete inattention to the bottom line. Concept Mapping is a great tool to help boards stay focused on the purposes of various grants and the reasons for making those grants.

Without any such systems of accountability, foundations can grow fat with staff, complex with work rules, sluggish in response to community needs, and ultimately ineffective except from the most superficial viewpoint. The salient features of foundations that overcome these challenges are: flat, nonhierarchical organizational structures, measurable outcomes, clear missions, a willingness to collaborate with others, and open lines of communication between the board and staff.

Foundation board members, however, are often part of the problem of failed accountability by encouraging a breakdown between the roles of the staff and themselves. It's fun to be a part-time program officer, and, in so doing, allow the staff to avoid accountability for efficiency and effectiveness. Autonomous boards that are broadly inclusive of all important stakeholders, focused on policy-level issues, and on the outcomes and impact of their work are likely to avoid the problems that come with stultifying bureaucracy and insulation.

Key Points To Remember:

- Concept Mapping is a graphic depiction of the grantmaker's beliefs, assumptions, and hopes for certain measurable outcomes resulting from a specific grant expenditure. Concept Mapping can provide a picture of assumed relationships in the past, present, or projected future.

- Grantmakers must frequently settle for an assumption of cause-and-effect based on imperfect knowledge unsupported by precise empirical evidence.

- The purpose of Concept Mapping is to communicate two viewpoints: (1) the approved viewpoint of "What to Do", and (2) the wider viewpoint of "What Not To Do" covering the strategic approaches that were considered but rejected.

- Autonomous boards that are broadly inclusive of all important stakeholders, focused on policy-level issues, and on the outcomes and impact of their work are likely to avoid the problems that come with stultifying bureaucracy and insulation.

- An early step in building a Concept Map is to complete a review of the literature about a topic of interest to the grantmaker. A literature review informs the grantmaker, identifies resources, notes best methods and failed methods, and forms a basis for grouping similar themes.

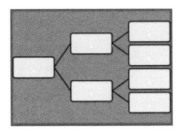

CHAPTER TWELVE

Other Uses of Concept Mapping

Mapping the Money

Concept Mapping is useful in a number of ways in addition to describing a set of assumed relationships or themes. It can also depict the intended or historic distribution of grant spending by the foundation or it can show the flow of money from a foundation to its grantees over time.

Spending on each grant can be added to a map in the appropriate category beginning at level seven or eight and then summed at each higher level all the way up to the mission in level one. For example, flash forward several years and the "Nurse Practitioner Project" could include several grants and contracts as shown below.

Tracing the "Nurse Practitioner Project" map, it is obvious that the single action step "Establish Recruitment Timetable" cost the grantmaker only $1,000. All five of the "Short-Term Recruitment" action steps, however, cost the foundation $216,000 and the entire "Human Capital" branch of the map including both short-term and long-term objectives cost almost $2 million.

Graphic 47: Nurse Practitioner Project Funding Example

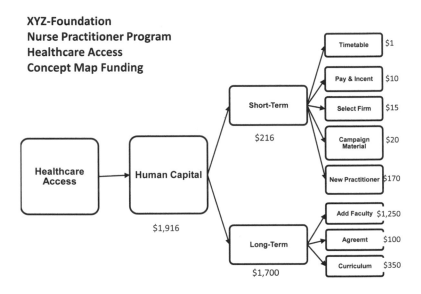

Graphic 48: Nurse Practitioner Project Funding Map Levels 3-7

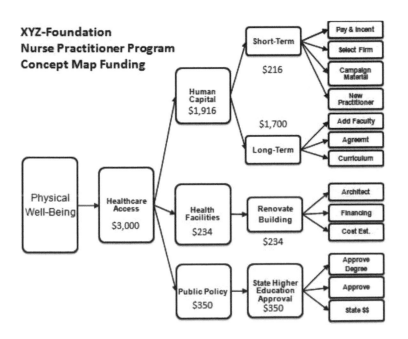

Rolling up the money map to level one "Mission" shows the grant money expended for all seven levels. Spending for the "Physical" "Well-Being of Children" is the sum of the five branches (Healthcare Access, Prevention, Early Screening, Food & Nutrition, and Toxicity & Hazards)

Money Mapping Strategies

In addition to graphically depicting the XYZ-Foundation spending for various levels, the same spending could be mapped for strategies such as "all Grantmaking", "all Operations", or "all Financial". A money mapping example of total XYZ-Foundation spending shows all spending of $9.8 million. A depiction of cumulative spending over each of ten years could produce a map at "Mission" (level 1) of roughly $100 million.

Graphic 49: Money Mapping for Levels 1 & 2

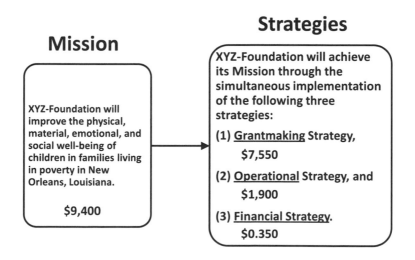

Mission

XYZ-Foundation will improve the physical, material, emotional, and social well-being of children in families living in poverty in New Orleans, Louisiana.

$9,400

Strategies

XYZ-Foundation will achieve its Mission through the simultaneous implementation of the following three strategies:

(1) <u>Grantmaking</u> Strategy,
   $7,550

(2) <u>Operational</u> Strategy, and
   $1,900

(3) <u>Financial Strategy</u>.
   $0.350

Money Mapping Budgets

The purpose of a business plan is to lay out the work to meet the mission that is anticipated a year into the future. Of necessity, such a business plan includes a budget for the XYZ-Foundation. Starting with level 7 (Action Plans), all spending planned for the year ahead can be mapped. Forward-looking money maps of anticipated spending provide an overall view that the reader can quickly understand.

Mapping Priorities

Concept Mapping is also useful in setting and demonstrating priorities. As an example, a map of the four goals of the XYZ-Foundation showed no preference for one goal over another. After debating their priorities and voting on the relative importance of each goal, the board arranged them in order.

Graphic 50: Board of Directors Prioritize Goals

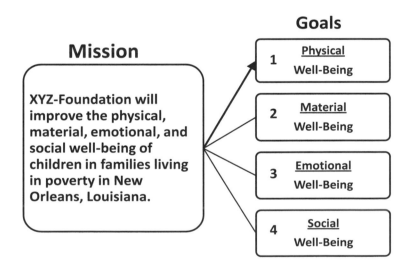

XYZ-Foundation used a vote-ranking procedure (included as an appendix in this book) with the board of directors to develop a prioritized list of grantmaking possibilities. After summing the votes of each board member at each map level, the priorities of the group are usually evident.

As an example, the board members of the XYZ-Foundation prioritized the four major zones of interest and discovered a strong sentiment to fund programs that focused on the physical well-being of children living in poverty as compared to funding the social well being of children.

Engaging Community

In the same way that a Concept Map can be used to establish funding priorities among board members, maps can also be used to solicit community input about the issues and challenges facing residents. Using focus groups, participants vote on the relative importance of funding one zone of interest over another.

As an example, the board-level ranking exercise described above was repeated among community attendees of three separate focus groups (one of grantees, one of the general public, and one of elected officials). The comparative results showed that the board was alone in ranking physical well-being as the most important.

Rather, the public ranked the zones of interest in almost reverse order and elected officials mostly agreed. This disparity of opinion led to a more sophisticated community educational series and listening projects before the public and the foundation were in agreement. After a few dozen interviews, the board of directors of XYZ-Foundation discovered that the affect of Hurricane Katrina on poor families was particularly hard on children. In response, families living in poverty in New Orleans (the target population) were very attentive to finding solutions to the emotional distress they were experiencing as compared to board members with more assets and coping capacities.

Graphic 51: Public and Elected Officials Prioritize Goals

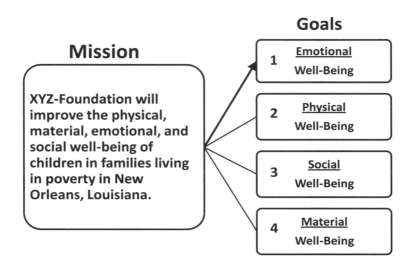

Using Concept Maps© to explain their priorities and to solicit more community input helped surface some very fundamental differences between the participants. It served as the basis for revisions to the goals that gained important new support from citizens and elected officials. Subsequently, maps were used as the basis for community presentations to describe and defend the funding choices made by the XYZ-Foundation.

Tyranny of Democratic Processes

This book contains a very useful approach to engaging groups of people in the community or on a board or committee in producing a topical consensus and a prioritized list (sees "Nominal Group Technique" Appendix One). One of the weaknesses of a group process is the fact that one or two participants can dominate the discussion. To combat the problem, a democratic process can be adopted wherein each participant is given a fair chance to participate. Strong personalities can usually be moderated with good facilitation but the "numbers" are inescapable in that a 51% consensus can be conclusive while still leaving 49% of the group dissatisfied with the outcome. In such an instance, the popular choice may be unrelated to the proper choice or the best choice for the community.

The chances of democratic tyranny happening are lessened when the leadership and organizers have fairly educated the participants on the positive an negative aspects of a wide range of possible outcomes. Tactful, observant, but firm facilitation also tends to reduce the chance of an unsupportable outcome. None the less, facilitators should be prepared to reconstitute a group which produces obviously aberrant results. If it is impossible or impractical to do so, the odd results should be watered down by either repeated exposure if in the same group, or repeated groups of differing composition.

From Snapshots to Movies

Concept Maps© represent a particular grantmaking pattern at one moment in time. They are static just like a home snap shot of a family. The people in the family are alive and dynamic and change whereas the snap shot is a fixed image of how they appeared in the past. Static images are extremely valuable for the information they contain but they are also limited because the reality of the situation is not static but changes very dynamically. This limitation can be minimized by taking a series of static images separated by time. For this reason, it is recommended that all grantmaking Concept Maps© be refreshed at least annually in the same cycle as the business plan.

Refreshing the maps keeps them current with the research literature and connects them to the changing preferences of the foundation or grantmaker and the environment in which they operate. As an example, in 2005, Hurricane Katrina forever changed the landscape of New Orleans. The needs of the community were dramatically different and these needs, in turn, changed the grantmaking programs of funders. Those grantmakers who continued to focus on pre-Katrina issues were living a static view of community needs which had changed in reality. Dynamic mapping is a process of continuous reinvention as both the literature and the environment change.

Dynamic mapping is to static concept mapping as movies are to still photographs. However, to keep mapping from becoming a tedious, overly time-consuming effort, maps should not be amended in real time throughout the year for several reasons. First, the literature and the environment change so quickly and frequently that even the most attentive grantmaker will be uninformed about important aspects. Second, one of the very useful attributes of Concept Mapping is that it tends to keep stakeholders informed of changes in the literature, the environment, and the preferences of the grantmaker. Constantly changing maps diminishes this vital communication and team-building capacity. Therefore, maps should only be updated once or twice each year with a preference for annually. In more complex situations where a grantmaker has a very broad mission with several maps, it is useful to consider rotating the renewal of maps through the year so that the work of renewal can be evenly distributed.

Most disciplines have a well-developed body of knowledge and a method of keeping adherents aware of changes and advances. Grantmakers are well-advised to subscribe to science and research-based journals in the disciplines in which they make grants or to which they devote staff resources. In addition to keeping abreast of developments through the literature, grantmakers should keep current by attending conferences and seminars. Maintaining a current knowledge base is not optional for grantmakers wanting maximum impact regardless of the use of Concept Mapping.

Each year, as grantmakers update their organization's Concept Maps©. they are also keeping their knowledge base current and are able to offer their communities, and grantees the latest evidence-based solutions to challenging conditions. Keeping the founder, board of directors, and the community aware of changes in the literature, environment, and preferences is relatively easy using Concept Maps© because the grantmaker makes it a habit of being up to date.

Going Full Circle: Reassessing

Many foundations maintain sophisticated evaluation systems to measure the progress of their grants in creating desired changes in their target population. At the same time, many program evaluations are overly complex and generate reams of indecipherable data. Evaluation does not have to be complicated or expensive to give grantmakers useful information about their grant outcomes, impacts, and effectiveness. It involves understanding the intent of the grant first. What is the desired outcome? Then, evaluation determines the best way to collect information from the grant program so that the funder can determine if progress is being made. Conceptually this is simple, but with over 35 different types of evaluation and complex data collection methods with equally complex statistical analysis, it can be confusing.

Concept Mapping works hand-in-hand with evaluation as a communication tool between grantees and foundations and among the actors within the foundation such as program officers, directors, and senior management. Properly mapped, each node of a project tree can be associated with at least one measurable indicator that can form the basis for a mutual agreement about what is to be done, and what effect is to be expected.

As Concept Maps© are refreshed, the literature examined, the environment observed, and grantmaker preferences determined, they can also convey what indicators will be identified and used as a basis for measurement. Management is often called upon to make major funding decisions on the basis of program evaluations. Therefore, a clearly defined indicator is very helpful to funders, grantees, and professional evaluators.

Obviously, the unit of measure is a negotiated point between the grantee and the funder but the example demonstrates the wide range of possible indicators or measures that can be applied. A simple qualitative outcome measure for a specific action plan can be the delivery of a report, a frequency count, or a test response. Higher up the tree, more sophisticated health indicators for a defined population can be adopted such as "practitioners per capita" or "visits per capita" that apply a ratio to a frequency.

These measures, while more sophisticated, are still process oriented. At the upper end of the tree, the physical well-being of children living in poverty can be measured by the use of original data drawn from randomized standard surveys of the target population. These indicators of population health can be very useful but are difficult to improve across a large population and they are influence by many more things than the programs captured in a single Concept Map. Such indicators provide a constant reminder that causality is very difficult to attribute to specific activities or programs even in the best of circumstances.

145

Using the "Nurse Practitioner Project" of the XYZ-Foundation as an example, several indicators can be associated with the various nodes of a Concept Map.

Graphic 52: Map With Suggested Indicators

XYZ-Foundation
Nurse Practitioner Program
Healthcare Access
Concept Map Indicators

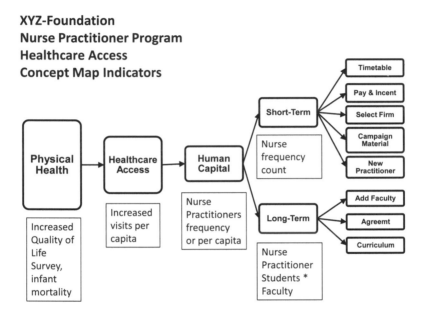

Occasionally, during the life of a grant or project, grantees should be required to report on their progress against the agreed upon indicator or output/outcome measure. A reporting requirement implies that the grantee is collecting sufficient data to measure progress and that achievements can be determined. However, the data collection technique should be settled with the grantee well before starting the project.

As time passes, the funded project collects and reports progress compared to the indicator or output/outcome measure agreed upon. Adjustments to the assumptions, design, or implementation of the program can be made on the basis of routine monitoring. Out of these quarterly or periodic reports of progress also come new opportunities for future funding, program improvement, and dissemination of findings.

The value of Concept Mapping as applied to the measurement of grantee progress is that each node on a map begs for a defined indicator or outcome. Grantees are held more accountable for their performance and funders are graphically reminded of the results they are expecting.

Grant Award Agreements

After a Concept Map has been designed and adopted and a series of indicators have been selected associated with each node, the intent of the funder in making a grant is clear. However, many grants are ineffective due to the failure of the funder to translate the intent of the grant into specific contract language and indicators that can be inserted into a grant award agreement.

Before issuing the first dollar to a grantee or contractor, foundations should discuss the entire range of the appropriate Concept Map with all parties in the project. This discussion is also a time for grantees to challenge the proposed indicator(s) and offer alternate measures that may already be collected or are easier to collect. This pre-award conference is also the time to clarify donor intent and to establish mutual expectations about the sequence of reporting and the content.

Key Points To Remember:

- Concept Mapping is a useful way to follow the money as funders issue grants and contracts to implement objectives and action plans.

- Cumulative funding can be tracked on Concept Maps© to observe funding trends by how money is applied on the ground.

- Tracking expenditures at the strategy level gives funders a feel for proportionality between grantmaking, operations, and finance.

- Concept Mapping is an excellent basis for setting priorities for funders.

- The community can be engaged in the early adoption of priorities by helping design Concept Maps© and ranking conflicting opportunities.

- Dynamic mapping adapts to changes in the environment over time.

- Concept Maps© can be associated with measurable indicators at each node and grant results can be monitored against selected elements of an evaluation plan.

- Foundations should discuss the entire range of the appropriate Concept Map with all parties in the project to reach a clear understanding of donor intent, measures, and monitoring.

CHAPTER THIRTEEN

Conclusion

A Picture Is Worth A Thousand Words

Supercharged Giving is a "how to" book for foundation professionals, donors, and grantmakers searching for ways to dramatically boost the impact of their giving. Strategic philanthropy and Concept Mapping are particularly more important in market downturns when every dollar counts. Two basic propositions are proposed: (1) that donors will increase their effectiveness by applying business-like approaches to strategize and implement their goals and objectives, and (2) that donor intent can be mapped as a picture, tied to indicators, and contractually imbedded in grant award agreements to help grantees and donors alike maintain a steady forward course over time.

Concept Mapping is a graphic or pictorial way to communicate quickly what a grant is, what is seeks to accomplish, the strategy being used, how it will be measured, and the relationship it has with other grants that make up a complete portfolio of work around a common theme. A picture is an easy way to show these relationships in a way that can be grasped quickly. As a short-hand language, Concept Mapping also reminds readers of different possible approaches to the solution of a particular problem that were considered but rejected. In so demonstrating, a map serves to frame the various strategies being used against competing theories and approaches making the chosen approach even more understandable.

149

Concept Mapping is a way to show graphically how various streams of donated money are attached to grant activities starting with the mission statement of the funder and ending up with action steps and budgets. Over several years of grantmaking, a single map can also display cumulative funding streams at a glance.

Using any of several tested consensus-building techniques, mapping can also serve as a basis for reaching agreement on grant strategies among groups such as the board of directors, family members, community residents, researchers, practitioners, etc. After participating in a map-based prioritization session, team members are more united in their work and tend to understand the big picture. This consensus builds stronger teams internally and externally and improves results.

Keeping It Simple

Concept Mapping and strategic thinking is not a more complicated way to do something that is otherwise simple or easy. Giving away money is never simple and it is only easy when the grantmaker is satisfied with good intentions rather than impact. Strategizing and mapping can produce big gains for grantmakers for the same money or it can boost impact in times of less money. It is precisely during financial downturns that a strategic approach is most important to grantmakers.

Concept Mapping is a simple way of creating an understandable grantmaking strategy and of communicating that strategy to grantees, the public and internal audiences. It is very robust and can fully describe the most technically challenging projects but it can also handle small, uncomplicated programs in easily understandable ways.

Supercharged Giving includes two examples for grantmakers. One is rather complex and includes a variety of grant products, processes, and styles known as the "Nurse Practitioner Project". The second is relatively simple in concept and easily communicated but deals with a complex subject known as the "Child Safety Project". The real-world range between these two examples is wide enough to serve most grantmaker needs and produces a quick boost in impact if for no other reason than it clarifies the expectations of the donor.

Money Up In Smoke

Many grantmakers are still mired in their historic giving patterns and can't imagine a better way to spend their charitable money. They also deal with and tolerate grantees that seem incapable of adhering to donor intent or following a grant award contract. These donors give money without demanding hard-driving, timely, measureable results from the nonprofits they support so they choose to let much of their hard-earned money (a very precious resource) go up in smoke. This undisciplined behavior is actually bad for grantmakers and grantees alike. It nurtures a culture of "good enough" and has the perverse effect of creating more dependency, not less. It is hard enough to gain even slight advantages against entrenched community challenges using every business-like approach to giving but grantmaking is often made even more ineffectual when donors telegraph to grantees a willingness to be satisfied with low-impact spending.

Every act of charity is not of equal importance in spite of an uncritical culture among donors and grantees. A very large proportion of donated money supports nonprofit organizations and causes that are not held accountable for their outcomes. This is probably more the fault of a sleepy philanthropic community than an unwilling or reluctant grantee. The proposal made in *Supercharged Giving* is to encourage donors to know precisely what they want to happen from their grants, why, and how the work will be done in a logical fashion that is measurable and connected to the donor's original reasoning. This way, their money is much less likely to go up in smoke.

Stick To The Knitting: The Tough Part

The passage of time is a double-edged blade for grantmakers. Some projects they fund can only have an impact if they are carried out over an extended length of time. However, grantmakers also have a tendency to tire of long-term projects focused on difficult challenges. Donors can fall prey to fads, smooth talking grantees, colleagues, and academics. In the face of all of these distractions, one of the most difficult things for donors is sticking to their knitting.

This is not to suggest that donors should give money to programs with an uncritical eye. More accurately, *Supercharged Giving* suggests that donors should only support grantees willing to work in a culture of intentional accountability over the long haul. In return, grantmakers should devote the necessary attention to researching and understanding their objectives as these diligent, hardworking nonprofits deserve.

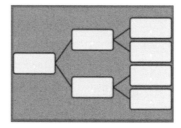

The End

APPENDIX
Nominal Group Technique

The ability of a group to reach consensus and to prioritize a list of topics is directly related to its ability to perform effectively. This appendix "Nominal Group Technique" is included in **Supercharged Giving** as a guide to help foundations and community groups reach agreement on what to do and how to do it. It is written as a series of slides so that users can simply adapt the material to a presentation and go straight to the content rather than building an approach from scratch.

Opening

Nominal Group Technique

How to reach group consensus and
prioritize opportunities.

philOptima, llc

Copyright, Philoptima, llc.
P. O. Box 53451
New Orleans, LA 70153
(504) 481-6281

Contact Philoptima, llc., to help facilitate your group discussions and to reach consensus on content and priorities.

The Nominal Group Technique (NGT) is an excellent approach to group discussions because it keeps every participant engaged, doesn't allow the group to be dominated by a few strong personalities, and produces a prioritized list of items. It can be used to reach consensus on a wide variety of subjects including objectives, goals, action plans, researched lists of interventions, community needs, opportunities, etc. For simplicity and consistency, this model is designed as an "Opportunity Exercise" which will produce a agreed upon list of opportunities in the community for a foundation to fund.

Preparation

> # Opportunities Exercise
> **Preparation:**
> Divide the participants into at least two groups.
>
> Supplies each: one easel, markers, tape or pins, 3X5 cards for voting.
>
> Recorder(s): Staff to serve as recorder. Staff may answer direct questions. No consultants!
>
> To Begin: select one Board member in each group to serve as "Reporter" to give the final group report.

Step One

> # Opportunities Exercise
>
> 1. Separately (without talking) think of a short title for each of the three most important health opportunities that you see.
>
>   Write each title in the upper left hand corner of a separate 3X5 card.
>
>   Limit one title per 3X5 card.

This exercise can produce a prioritized list of from three items to as many as ten items. Experience supports the greatest cohesion of the group is tilted in favor of a short list with the most desirable being between three and seven items.

Using the 3x5 cards, write one title for one opportunity per card. Below is a sample Title Card and a sample card completed for Neighborhood Clinics.

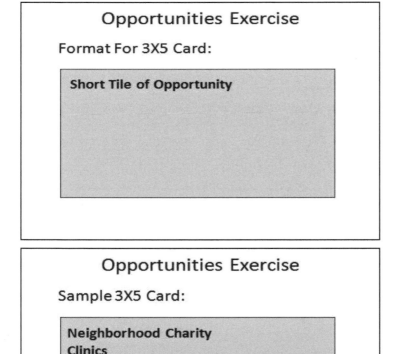

Next, the topic should be described in sufficient detail to be clear and unduplicated as each table participant is invited to discuss his/her next highest priority later in the process.

Step Two

Opportunities Exercise

2. Next, write a short description in the center of each 3X5 card that defines each opportunity title.

Opportunities Exercise

Format For 3X5 Card:

Tile of Opportunity

Brief description of the opportunity.

Opportunities Exercise

Sample 3X5 Card:

Neighborhood Charity Clinics

> **Emphasize ambulatory care, wellness, prevention, health promotion, and chronic disease management in a network of neighborhood charity clinics.**

Step Three

Opportunities Exercise

3. Finally, write the <u>rank</u> "1" for your most important opportunity in the upper right hand corner of the 3X5 card.

   1 = Highest Rank

   Then, rank the other two opportunities as "2" and "3".

Opportunities Exercise

Format For 3X5 Card:

Tile of Opportunity   Your **Rank** for this opportunity.

1=Highest

Brief description of the opportunity.

Opportunities Exercise

Sample 3X5 Card:

Neighborhood Charity Clinics   1

Emphasize ambulatory care, wellness, prevention, health promotion, and chronic disease management in a network of neighborhood charity clinics.

Now that each participant has submitted to the group a "first choice" topic and description, they can move to a facilitated discussion of the list.

Discussion

Opportunities Exercise

4. Explain your most important opportunity to the other table members (without lobbying).

   Go around the table allowing each participant to share his/her highest priority opportunity until all "first choices" have been discussed.

   Staff will record each participant's first choice on the easel-sheet.

Repeat the cycle with the "second" and then the "third" priority lists of the individual participants (up to ten cycles).

Opportunities Exercise

5. Sequentially, go around the table and disclose and record on the easel-tablet each participant's "second priority", and then "third priority. Mount each sheet on the wall.

6. Consolidate similar topics so that each opportunity is unique. Don't write on the wall!

7. On a separate sheet, each table member should rank the entire final list of opportunities from the table from "1" to "**"

Opportunities Exercise

8. Take a short break and all votes for each
    opportunity will be totaled for each table and a
    new table priority list written.

9. Each table Reporter will announce and explain
    the <u>top three</u> table priorities from most to least
    important.

10. <u>Finished</u>. Staff will draft a list of top
    opportunities for distribution to the members
    and for consideration by the Board of Directors.

Opportunities Exercise

8. Take a short break and all votes for each
    opportunity will be totaled for each table and a
    new table priority list written.

9. Start again on the next Zone of Interest,
    discipline, or theme.

This "Nominal Group Techinque" is a very useful approach to reaching consensus and for prioritizing any type of list of topics. It is helpful in community discussions and in reaching consensus among the members of the Board of Directors or staff.

SUPERCHARGED GIVING
END NOTES

1. Gothe, J. W. v. (1808). <u>Faust, The Tragedy, Part One</u>.

Something that is "Faustian" refers to a wider interpretation of the events of Faust by Johann Wolfgang von Goethe.

2. Madoff, R. D. (2008). Dog Eat Your Taxes? <u>New York Times</u>. New York.

American taxpayers subsidize the whims of the rich and fulfill their fantasies of immortality by allowing them to gain tax advantages by making a gift to a private foundation and then allowing the donor to control the "donated" assets for many generations. While some choose to contribute to broad public goals, the law does not require it. The law requires foundations to spend a minimum of 5% of their assets a year, thus helping ensure their perpetual existence, and their donors' immortality. However, because a dollar spent today is worth more than a dollar spent several years from now, in many cases, the sum of payments made over time never equals the value of the original principal.

3. Buchanan, P. (2002). <u>Indicators of Effectiveness: Understanding and Improving Foundation Performance</u>. Cambridge, MA, The Center for Effective Philanthropy.

Foundation leaders are increasingly concerned about measuring foundation performance and effectiveness. It is very difficult and costly to measure the final social benefit of a grantmaker. Performance measurement models typically rely on one of two approaches: formal evaluations of outputs, outcomes, and impacts, and much simpler and less directly related studies of administrative costs, efficiencies, and investment results.

4. Prager, D. J. (2003). <u>Organizing Foundations for Maximum Impact: A Guide to Effective Philanthropy</u>. Washington, DC, The Aspen Institute.

Dr. Prager summarizes the opportunities and dilemmas of philanthropy by describing the strengths and weaknesses of the nonprofit foundation model relative to the natural business environment. He notes the differences between giving away money and investing financial support in effective nonprofits to create important changes in social conditions. The primary difference between effective philanthropy and ineffective philanthropy rests on keeping the ultimate social goals in mind versus various bureaucratic outputs and systematically pursuing success while avoiding the allure of new, unproven initiatives. The author makes a strong case for foundation self-assessment and rigorous evaluation of outcomes and impacts.

5. Friedman, L. et. al. (2004). <u>Charity, Philanthropy, and Civility in American History</u>. London, England, Cambridge University Press.

The authors demonstrate that philanthropic activities cannot substitute for collective public action to deal with major social problems. Professional historians address the dominant issues and theories to explain the history of American philanthropy and its role in American society. The overarching premise is that philanthropic activity in America has its roots in the desires of individuals to impose their visions of societal ideals, or conceptions of truth, upon society.

6. Dowie, M. (2001). <u>American Foundations: An Investigative History</u>. Cambridge, MA, The MIT Press.

Foundation staff and trustees spend thousands of working hours struggling to define values and concepts.... in the hopes of identifying a social need or problem that fits both the intention of their original donor and their own perceptions of how to use money to enhance the public good. Their collective imagination has created some of the best and worst institutions in America. Dowie urges that foundations need to adopt democratic reforms (like citizen trustees, grantee advisory boards, and strong social agendas) to justify their influence.

7. Wooster, M. M. (2006). <u>Great Philanthropic Mistakes</u>. Washington, D.C., Hudson Institute.

The author describes several major philanthropic mistakes including the Carnegie and Rockefeller supported "Flexner Report" (Abraham Flexner) the most controversial recommendation from which was the full-time employment of medical school faculties (the first of which was Johns Hopkins Medical School). Many supposedly fly-by-night medical schools closed; making access even more difficult and particularly harmful to women and minorities entering medicine and thus also for treatment of those larger populations.

The Albert and Mary Lasker Foundation "war on cancer" in which they lobbied for and got a greatly expanded federal role in disease treatment spending $5.2billion between 1969-1978 with no discernable effect, thus arguing that limitless money may not be an answer.

The Rockefeller and Ford Foundations sparked, funded, and then shut down major population control programs from the 1960's to the 1980's having decided essentially that such projects were ineffective and without merit.

In the war on poverty, Ford Foundation funded militancy and a dramatic expansion of the welfare state under Lyndon Johnson without any data-driven evaluation of more than 200 programs and no demonstrable effect on poverty.

The Carnegie Foundation funded public television twice and the Ford Foundation once to create noncommercial television of a higher quality than that supported by other forms of income. Arguably, A&E, the History Channel, Bravo, Discovery, and American Movie Classics offering cultural programming and science documentaries weigh against the theory of public television, leaving today's PBS irrelevant and expensive.

The Ford Foundation (1967-68) funded several efforts to decentralize public schools as one means to combat racism. It only created additional bureaucracies and did not improve student performance while fueling racial discord.

The MacArthur Foundation funded "genius awards" to free bright people from bureaucracy. It was decentralized, revived the concept of individual grants. Against the question of what was accomplished that would not have been, there is little evidence of success but the program is now institutionalized and impervious to serious change.

The Annenburg Foundation funded $500 million to reform public schools matched by another 50% ($250 million) by other foundations with only modest, incremental changes in how public schools in nine cities are governed, operated, and measured. Teachers, unions, boards, elected officials, and principals all nine cities found reasons to resist change. Expanded kindergarten was a positive but little else.

8. Fleishman, J. L. (2007). <u>The Foundation: A Great American Secret (How Private Wealth is Changing the World)</u>. New York, Public Affairs (Perseus Books Group).

9. Sage_Foundation (2008). The Russell Sage Foundation: Visiting Scholars Program.

10. VERA_Institute (2008). Criminal Justice, Sentencing, and Corrections.

11. Schambra, W. (2008). <u>Strategic Philanthropy: A Presentation</u>. Chicago Grantmakers for Effective Organizations.

In a sample of foundations that are among the nation's largest, and sufficiently confident in their grantmaking prowess, foundations are becoming ever more absorbed in technique and calibration, ever more focused on internal operations, even as they tell themselves they're honing better instruments to bring about external change. Very few could describe their work using any sort of hypothesized causal connections, much less causal connections that might reach to the roots of our problems.

12. Buchanan, P. (2008). The Mission of the Center for Effective Philanthropy.

The mission of the Center for Effective Philanthropy (CEP) is to provide data and create insight so philanthropic funders can better define, assess, and improve their effectiveness and impact.

13. Frumkin, P. (2006). <u>Strategic Giving: The Art and Science of Philanthropy</u>. Chicago, University of Chicago.

Philanthropy is complex precisely because it is individualistic. Charity and philanthropy are different and overlapping concepts. Developing and implementing clear and empirically based strategies to achieve well defined outcomes is critical to success in the private business world and the public sector as well. Donations are more driven by mission and passion than efficiency or even effectiveness. The author questions whether any strategies, tactics, schemes, and dreams actually improves the effectiveness of foundation giving or increases social impact.

14. Porter, M. E., Kramer, M.R. (1999). "Philanthropy's New Agenda: Creating Value." Harvard Business Review (November/December 1999): 121-130.

Foundations have an obligation to add value to philanthropy compared to direct immediate giving. The immediate social benefit of a direct gift from the donor to the charity is 250% of the lost tax revenue. Foundations add two additional layers of costs through the costs of operating the foundation and through the administrative reporting burden added to the grantee. Therefore foundations must add value through: (1) selecting the best charities to fund, (2) signaling other funders to leverage more funding to the best charities, (3) improving grantee performance, and (4) advancing the state of practice for the entire field.

15. Gertner, J. (2008). For Good Measure. The New York Times Magazine. The Money Issue: 62-66, 74.

Foundations are increasingly using "metrics" to measure the performance of their donations. Spending more doesn't necessarily increase the impact of a program. The current evaluation wave is about ten years old and has evolved to include logic modeling and theory of change. These efforts tend to also support an understanding of the cost-benefit of a program. The question is "do these methods push philanthropy to adopt unrealistic expectations?" Such approaches will give little attention to the arts for example.

16. Rojas, R. R. (2000). "A Review of Models for Measuring Organizational Effectiveness Among For-Profit and Nonprofit Organizations." Nonprofit Management & Leadership 11(1): 97-104.

17. Orosz, J., C.Philips and L. Wyatt Knowlton (2003). Agile Philanthropy: Understanding Foundation Effectiveness. Grand Rapids, MI, Grand Valley State University: Dorothy A. Johnson Center for Philanthropy and NonProfit Leadership.

The model for foundation effectiveness developed by Orosz et al. suggests that a foundation's internal processes also contribute to the ultimate success or failure of its grantees. Their model identifies three internal foundation "levers" that contribute to the outcomes of grantees and ultimately to foundation effectiveness. These internal levers include "people, priorities and processes".

18. Harrell, B., and Richard Culbertson (2004). The Performance of Health Conversion Foundations. New Orleans, Louisiana, Tulane University Press.

19. Bruce, A., and Ken Langdon (2000). Strategic Thinking. New York, NY, Dorling Kindersley.

20. Kramer, M. (2001). "Strategic Confusion." Foundation News & Commentary(May/June): 40-45.

The author believes that the development of a theory of change is one of the core principles of "strategic philanthropy"; a foundation's theory of change reflects its beliefs about "how to create change in society".

21. Morris, A. J. (2004). A Survey of Theories of Change Within Philanthropy. <u>School of Public Administration</u>, Grand Valley State University.

Theory of change may best be described as the underlying assumptions of what a particular problem is and ideas on how to solve the problem. The author suggests that the field of philanthropy has adopted the term theory of change as its own, giving it its own special twist to the meaning of the term.

22. Stauber, K. (2001). "Mission-Driven Philanthropy: What Do We Accomplish and How Do We Do It?" <u>NonProfit and Voluntary Sector Quarterly</u> vol. 30(no. 2): 393-399.

The author describes what historically has served as the Northwest Area Foundation's theory of change: a theory that was "adopted from the Carnegie–Rockefeller–Ford model of philanthropy" (Stauber, 2001, p. 394).

23. Weiss, H., J. Coffman and M. Bohan-Baker (2002). <u>Strategic Analysis. In Evaluation's Role in Supporting Inititative Sustainability</u>. Boston, MA, Harvard University.

Theory of change does not make a particularly good case for objectivity within grantmaking; instead it highlights the subjectivity of grantmaking. Typically a theory of change is based on a combination of objective evidence drawn from research or experience, and subjective opinion and personal ideology.

24. Weiss, C. H. (1998). <u>Evaluation: Methods for Studying Programs and Policies</u>. Upper Saddle River, NJ, Prentice-Hall, Inc.Theory of change is the "set of beliefs that underlie action" (Weiss, H., 1998, p. 55).

25. Mintzberg, H. and J. Quinn (1996). <u>The Strategy Proc-</u>

ess: Concepts, Contexts and Cases, Prentice Hall.

26. Porter, M. E. (2008). "The Five Competitive Forces That Shape Strategy." Harvard Business Review 86(1): 79-93.

The seminal work on this theory was first published by Porter in 1979, "How Competitive Forces Shape Strategy". The five forces are: rivalry among existing competitors, the threat of new entrants, the threat of substitute products or services, the bargaining power of buyers, and the bargaining power of suppliers.

27. Peters, T. J. and R. H. Waterman (1982). In Search of Excellence: Lessons From America's Best Run Companies. New York, NY, Harper and Row.

The eight attributes of excellence are: (a) a bias for action, (b) being close to customers, (c) autonomy and entrepreneurship, (d) being productive through people, (e) an active shared value system among all levels, (f) a simple and lean staff, (g) simultaneous loose-tight properties, and (h) a resistance to conglomeracy and a focus on what is known or done best ("sticking to the knitting").

28. Frumkin, P. (2002). On Being Nonprofit: A Conceptual and Policy Primer. Cambridge, MA, Marvard University Press.

The author identifies four core functions of the nonprofit sector: promoting political and civic engagement, delivering critical services, providing a vehicle for social entrepreneurship, and acting as an outlet for the expression of faith and values. Fulfilling a nonprofits mission and enhancing its bottom line are two different and often incompatible goals. The author provides comparative advantages and disadvantages faced by nonprofits. On the one hand nonprofits can use the non-distribution constraint to establish trust with clients in ways that for-profits cannot. On the other hand, nonprofits suffer a natural efficiency disadvantage owing to unclear channels of accountability, often inadequate funding for infrastructure, and forced inattention to bottom-line issues.

The salient characteristics of an effective nonprofit organization are the tendency to (1) collaborate with other organizations, (2) diversify income sources, (3) measure outcomes, (4) build flat, non-hierarchical, team-based workforces with open communications, and (5) keep clear lines of communication and responsibility between staff and the board of directors.

29. Brest, P. a. H. H. (2008). <u>Money Well Spent: A Strategic Plan for Smart Philanthropy</u>. New York, NY, Bloomberg Press.

30. Harrell, B. (2008). <u>Performance Pacing: How to Measure and Benchmark Your Foundation</u>. New Orleans, Philoptima, llc.

31. Kimbell, D. a. T. N. (2006). Separating the Roles of Chairman and Chief Executive: Looking at Both Sides of the Debate.

Following the corporate scandals of the early 2000s, many governance observers and commentators in the United States began to discuss whether, in order to avert such crises in the future, boards should separate the roles of chairman and chief executive officer, a practice common to governance models in the United Kingdom, much of the rest of Europe, as well as Canada and Australia.

While some in the US embrace the notion of separating the roles of chairman and CEO, others reject the division of power. The authors conclude that the statistical evidence suggests that there is a steady tide of reform in the US with the most significant being the emergence of a strong independent lead or presiding director possibly assuming the duties of the chairman. However, they conclude by suggesting that there is mutual respect and merit in both models. One side is not better than the other — just different — and both should continue to learn from the experiences of the other.

32. Buchanan, P. (2004). <u>Foundation Governance: The CEO Viewpoint</u>. Cambridge, MA, The Center for Effective Philanthropy.

Recent corporate governance reforms have prompted a number of changes in private foundations including the formation of independent audit committees, requiring the CEO to sign off on the final tax return, and strengthened conflict of interest policies. These moves tend to increase transparency. Five variables were good predictors of the view of the CEO that their Board was an effective Board, including: the Board is involved in assessing the overall performance of the organization, the Board brings thought provoking and important matters to the attention of the CEO, the Board discusses governance issues raised in the popular press, fewer donor family members serve on the Board, and the Board actively represents the organization to the public. These Boards also meet more frequently than those viewed as ineffective and they are engaged in setting overall strategy, measuring social impact, and the individual members contribute expertise to the organization. About half of all respondent organizations compensate some or all of their Board members and the CEOs of organizations that compensate directors also tend to view their Boards as more engaged. Term limits exist in 50% of all respondents but are poorly enforced.

33. Rossi, P., and Howard Freeman, and Mark Lipsey (1999). <u>Evaluation: A Systematic Approach</u>. London, Sage Publications.

For the purpose of evaluating social programs, evaluation is the use of social research procedures to systematically investigate the effectiveness of social intervention programs through the diagnosis of social problems, conceptualization and design of an evaluation model, implementation, administration and outcomes including efficiency.

34. Kaplan, R. S. (2002). "The Balanced Scorecard and Nonprofit Organizations." <u>The Balanced Scorecard Report</u> November: 1-4.

35. Center_for_Effective_Philanthropy (2008). Multi-Dimensional Assessment Process.

36. Lehfeldt, M. (2008). The Challenge Facing American Philanthropy. <u>The Richmond Times Dispatch</u>. Richmond, VA.

The author summarizes his view of the passions of foundations noting that they are at the top of their game when they have the guts to take on tough challenges -- when they are prepared to break ranks with their own traditional guidelines, with their peers, and sometimes even with public opinion to tackle issues and problems from which it would have been much easier to turn their eyes. More foundations, which are all too often in his opinion characterized by their cautiousness, need to demonstrate vision and courage. The ethical choice before foundations, in the opinion of the author, is whether they will continue to be satisfied with slapping bandages on the needs of the poor or whether they are going to change the policies and practices that help perpetuate poverty. He concludes that it's all about courage.

37. Carver, M. (2008). "Ten Questions To Ask When Invited To Join A Board." Nonprofit World 26, No. 5(September-October): 20-22.1.

38. Bolman, L. G. and T. E. Deal (1997). Reframing Organizations: Artistry, Choice, and Leadership. San Francisco, CA, Jossey-Bass.

The basic assumptions of the structural perspective are that organizations are rational institutions whose primary purpose is to accomplish established objectives.

39. Harrell, B., and Richard Culbertson (2006). "Size Matters: Why Big Foundations Perform Poorly." Philanthropy 20 (4): 15-16.

40. Donaldson, L. (2001). The Contingency Theory of Organizations. Thousand Oaks, CA, Sage Publications, Inc.

41. Dudley, L. S. (2003). "Bureaucracy." Encyclopedia of Public Administration and Public Policy DOI: 10.1081/E-EPAP-120010952(03/01/2003): 126 - 129.

42. Casey, C. (2004). "Bureaucracy Re-enchanted?" Organization 11(1): 59-81.

43. Buhner, R. and P. Moller (1985). "The Information Context of Corporate Disclosures of Divisionalization Decisions." Journal of Management Studies 22: 309-326.

Explores alternative performance indicators such as "market" rather than accounting measures.

44. Chandler, A. D., Jr. (1962). Strategy and Structure: Chapters in the History of the American Industrial Enterprise. Cambridge, MA, MIT Press.

Organizations tend to avoid adopting the necessary structures demanded by the environment until there is a crisis in performance.

45. Blau, P. M. and P. A. Schoenherr (1971). <u>The Structure of Organizations</u>. New York, NY, Basic Books.

Size is an important contingency factor that effects organizational structures. To cope with different environments, organizations create different specialized structures. Structure may be thought of as increases in structural sophistication and complexity.

46. Child, J. (1973). "Parkinson's Progress: Accounting for the Number of Specialists in Organizations." <u>Administrative Science Quarterly</u> 18: 328-348.

47. Hall, D. J. and M. D. Saias (1980). "Strategy Follows Structure!" <u>Strategic Management Journal</u> 1: 149-163.

48. Ostrower, F. (2004). Attitudes and Practices Concerning Effective Philanthropy. Washington D.C., The Urban Institute: 1-15.

The author reports that most foundations indicate that their grantee relations are good or excellent. Among those that reported excellent, only 29% had solicited anonymous or non-anonymous grantee feedback through interviews, surveys, or focus groups. The finding raises questions about the basis upon which foundations make any judgment about their relationships.

49. Barnard, F. (1921). "One Look is Worth A Thousand Words." <u>Printer's Ink</u>.

It is believed that the modern use of the phrase "a picture is worth 1,000 words" stems from an article by Fred R. Barnard in the advertising trade journal Printers' Ink, promoting the use of images in advertisements that appeared on the sides of streetcars. The December 8, 1921 issue carries an ad entitled, "One Look is Worth A Thousand Words."

50. Tufte, E. R. (1997). Visual Explanations: Images and Quantities, Evidence and Narrative. Cheshire, CT, Graphics Press.

The core of Tufte's work documents how to best display different forms of information.

51. Holmes, N., Mark Reiter and Richard Sandomir (2007). The Enlightened Bracketologist: The Final Four of Everything, Bloomsbury Publishing.

Nigel Holmes has written six books on various aspects of information design and the use of pictures and graphs to convey meaning.

52. Bird, R. J. (2003). Chaos and Life: Complexity and Order in Evolution and Thought. New York, NY, Columbia University Press.

The butterfly effect is a phrase that encapsulates the more technical notion of sensitive dependence on initial conditions in chaos theory. Small variations of the initial condition of a dynamical system may produce large variations in the long term behavior of the system. So this is sometimes presented as esoteric behavior, but can be exhibited by very simple systems: for example, a ball placed at the crest of a hill might roll into any of several valleys depending on slight differences in initial position. What at first appears to be random in a chaotic system may not be.

53. Hilborn, R. C. (2004). "Sea gulls, butterflies, and grasshoppers: A brief history of the butterfly effect in nonlinear dynamics." American Journal of Physics 72: 425–427.

Due to nonlinearities in weather processes, a butterfly flapping its wings in Tahiti can, in theory, produce a tornado in Kansas. This strong dependence of outcomes on very slightly differing initial conditions is a hallmark of the mathematical behavior known as chaos.

54. Wikipedia (2008). Root Cause Analysis.

Root cause analysis (RCA) is a class of problem solving methods aimed at identifying the root causes of problems or events. The practice of RCA is predicated on the belief that problems are best solved by attempting to correct or eliminate root causes, as opposed to merely addressing the immediately obvious symptoms. By directing corrective measures at root causes, it is hoped that the likelihood of problem recurrence will be minimized. However, it is recognized that complete prevention of recurrence by a single intervention is not always possible. Thus, RCA is often considered to be an iterative process, and is frequently viewed as a tool of continuous improvement.

55. LaBrosse, M. (2008). "Do You Know Where Your Goals Are?" Nonprofit World 26, No.5(September-October): 15.

56. Ashton, L. (2008). Effects of Money and Staff Skills on Grant Outcomes. New Orleans: 4.

57. Boyne, G. A. (2003). "Public and Private Management: What's the Difference?" Journal of Management Studies 39 (1).

Critics argue that differences between public and private organizations are so great that business practices should not be transferred to the public sector.

SPECIAL BONUS REPORT

Size Matters:

Why Big Foundations Perform Poorly

Typically, in order to accomplish their objectives, grant making foundations rely heavily on nonprofit grantee organizations. As practicing foundation and nonprofit executives and academics, we thought, therefore, that all foundations should be very interested in understanding their relationships with grantees in order to improve their own performance. Surprisingly, most foundations do not ask grantees for feedback about key areas of their operations that influence their relationships. Were they to ask, large foundations might discover that they are not performing near as well as they think. Whether this reluctance to ask the tough questions comes from arrogance, skepticism, or fear of accountability, the result is that valuable input is often ignored.

Under the auspices of the Southeastern Council of Foundations, we systematically surveyed 230 grantees of 30 health legacy foundations in the south and found that large foundations tend to earn lower performance results than smaller foundations. Assuming that the relationship between grantees and health legacy foundations is no different, our findings may be of interest to other family, community, and independent foundations. For the purpose of this study, large foundations were defined as those with assets greater than $100 million. They are viewed by grantees as less effective foundations and they show several consistent weaknesses. They are criticized for wandering into fields in which they have little or no expertise, for being less flexible in responding to grantees and for rigidly enforcing their operating rules. These large foundations are also criticized for not taking risks or encouraging experimentation. Smaller foundations, defined as those with assets less than $100 million, tend to make quicker decisions, place greater value on their grantees, show more flexibility with their grant making rules, and are more tolerant when circumstances change. All of these factors in combination lead to a perception among grantees of higher performance.

Study Design

Health legacy foundations hold the residual assets from the sale of nonprofit assets to for-profit companies. Typically, they invest the sale proceeds and make grants to other nonprofits. Thirty southeastern health legacy foundations responded to a survey in 2004 designed to document several of their important organizational characteristics. Additionally, a random group of more than 230 grantees graded the performance of these same foundations using a sixteen-item questionnaire modified specifically for nonprofit foundation grantees. Peters and Waterman (1982) identified the original indicators of high-performance businesses in their best-selling book "In Search of Excellence", and Sharma, designed the original business-oriented questionnaire.

Findings & Conclusions

Low performing foundations are often larger foundations. Size seems to beget few performance benefits. On average, the larger the foundation, the greater the likelihood that it is a low-performer. This finding throws into question the bureaucracy, hierarchy, and complex work rules used by large foundations as they attempt to add value to their philanthropy. The tradeoff between a dollar spent on staff and a dollar given directly to a grantee is a difficult balance. Large foundations are characterized by large staffs, which, in turn, may tend to justify themselves and ever larger staffs. Grantee responses indicate that the foundation staffs add less value than increased program funding.

Large foundations earn very low marks for their inflexibility. These foundations may place more importance on the grantee following the rules than on having an impact. This frustrates grantees and goes hand-in-hand with large foundation staffs. Since foundations do not have a widely supported method of measuring success, they may be retreating to the predictable activity of bureaucracy, enforcing process rules. Increased hierarchy may also tend to enforce rigidity as each successive layer of staff has less latitude to be flexible with grant rules.

The eminent sociologist Max Weber (1947) observed that bureaucratization is an inevitable, and in some aspects even desirable, development of modern organizational life. As organizations increase in size and complexity, adherence to impersonal rules and their uniform application increase as well. Legal authority emanating from the top of

178

the organization becomes a defining characteristic of large organizations.

As a predictable consequence of the process of bureaucratization, large foundations are unwilling to experiment. All of the talk among foundations about taking risks seems to disappear among big foundations. Smaller foundations are more willing to jump into risky projects. Since one of the touted strengths of private foundations is that they can afford to take on risky projects, it seems that the fear of failure is an important grant-making disincentive that neutralizes this theoretical strong point in large foundations. Grantees believe that large foundations create an atmosphere that systematically dampens innovation. This is predictable behavior on the part of foundation boards as their fiduciary pressure to conserve the corpus of the foundation exceeds the pressure for desired programmatic results.

Large foundations perform even more poorly as they add staff and decentralize their decision-making. Mintzberg (1989) observed that as organizations increase in size, they adopt mechanisms to improve performance. One mechanism to improve operations is to push decision-making further down into the hierarchy. However, when this happens among foundations, performance actually falls. Focus groups of grantees explain that the act of decentralization in foundations merely adds layers to each decision and slows things down. Foundations may be decentralizing in name only. Whether the staff of a foundation is too defensive to make decisions, or too browbeaten by their boards every time a mistake happens, is open to debate. Grantees, however, see more foundation staff as an impediment and, perhaps, as wasted money.

Large foundations tend to forget old friends. When a grant ends, it appears that large foundations declare victory and move on. Grantees criticize foundations for not following up on their programs after the end of the grant. Few large foundations visit former grantee organizations to see if their funding left any lasting impact. Some grantees view this as disinterest, others as the product of values. Large foundations may value funding more than relationships and all of this talk about "partnership" may just be talk.

Grantees think that large foundations often make grants in fields in which they have little or no expertise. Perhaps they are easily bored with one field of work or easily defeated by some very durable social problems, but, foundations seem to be constantly looking for the next new thing. Grantees are uncertain about how to confront a funder with poorly conceived projects but strongly held notions of cause and effect. Smaller, high-performing foundations score better for "sticking to their knitting".

Only grantees appear to be required to follow the rules. Often, large foundations do not stick to their grant guidelines for pet projects. Sometimes grantees see funding decisions that are strictly the result of a strong personality at the foundation. Rules change. Grantees are then confused. Is it who they know or what they know that is funded? A foundation composed of several different personality cults is a foundation prone to break its own rules. They may also be violating their publicized policies in favor of the latest fad. Grantees give low scores in either event.

On the other hand, high-performing, smaller foundations earn higher scores for things that are important to grantees. In particular, these foundations seem to adhere closely to their stated values. They hire employees that exemplify their values, and they let their values drive the direction of their organization. Smaller, high-performing foundations also pay attention to their grantees and listen to their opinions. They believe in their grantees and support them emotionally and intellectually as well as financially. High performers give personalized attention to their grantees. This may explain why they are often smaller foundations. High performers also encourage innovation and creativity, unlike the larger, low-performing foundations. The high-performance foundations seem to be less fixated on following the rules and more flexible. Lastly, high-performance foundations have lean operations with small staffs and efficient management. This is in direct contrast to the low-performing larger foundations.

The question that large foundations should be asking, is: "how can we retain the advantages of size (for instance in fund management, capacity building, durability, or research) while cultivating the strengths of a smaller organization (such as flexibility, close relationships, and quick decisions)? Why not ask your grantees?

Published: Philanthropy, Vol.XX,No.4, July/August 2006, p.15-16

Byron R. Harrell, Sc.D.
Chief Science Officer
Philoptima, llc.
Byron R. Harrell is the Chief Science Officer of Philoptima,llc. and President of a large health legacy foundation in New Orleans.

Richard A. Culbertson, Ph.D.
Professor
Health Systems Management, Tulane University

Richard Culbertson is Associate Professor in the Department of Health Systems Management in the School of Public Health and in the Department of Family Medicine at Tulane University.

Order copies of **Supercharged Giving**. Visit our website:

www.superchargedgiving.com

Quick Order Form

To order more copies of this book, visit our web site, fax, or mail your credit card information.

Email orders: www.superchargedgiving.com or www.Philoptima.org

Postal Orders: Mail the order form to:
　　　　　　Philoptima, llc
　　　　　　P.O. Box 53451
　　　　　　New Orleans, LA 70153

Fax Orders: Fax the order form to 1-800-497-6605

　　　　Please send me a copy of Super Charged Giving

Name:_____

Address: _____

City: _____ State:_____ Zip:_____

Email address:_____ Telephone No._____

Credit card number:_____; Expiration date:_____

Name on credit card:_____

Or mail or fax this quick order form for prompt service.
Consult with Dr. Byron Harrell
Call (504) 481-6281 or send email: bharrell@philoptima.org

Dr. Byron Harrell is available for speaking engagements, seminars, presentations, and consulting services. He has provided foundations and donors with the following:

- Review of grantmaking process, products, and styles.
- Assessment of grantmaking strengths and weaknesses.
- Implementation of a strategic grantmaking approach.
- Implementation of concept mapping for grantmaking.
- Program evaluation design.
- Creative planning cycles.
- Board retreat facilitation.

How the Open Innovation System Works

Give your donations new impact through affordable web-based research.

Philoptima, llc.™, helps foundations, donors, and other grant makers clearly describe a community challenge and create a cash prize to spur innovative ideas to help solve the problem. Using the system of Open Innovation Philanthropy, prize makers can attack a wide variety of community problems by connecting them to consultants, researchers, and experts offering best-practice solutions using an internet-based open innovation platform. In a second challenge phase, Philoptima, llc.,™ also helps connect funders to nonprofits with specific implementation skills in a local community.

Using the Open Innovation Philanthropy system is easy. Donors and prize makers looking for competitive ideas from a wide array of consultants and researchers need look no further for quick, cost effective responses to the problems and challenges that you describe.

- Join Philoptima by registering at no cost to you.
- Complete our special Problem Statement Form.
- Set the deadline for responses.
- Arrange payment of your prize and we post it to the web.

Funders can't lose. If you don't like the responses from our consultants and researchers after the deadline, you get 100% of your money back